AN ACADEMIC WRITING TEXT

VISIONS

EMILY LITES JEAN LEHMAN

Illustrations by Marj McMinn

PRENTICE HALL REGENTS   Englewood Cliffs, New Jersey 07632

Library of Congress Cataloging-in-Publication Data

Lites, Emily,
    Visions : an academic writing text / Emily Lites, Jean Lehman.
      p. 208
    Includes bibliographical references.
    ISBN 0-13-946070-5
    1. English language—Textbooks for foreign speakers. 2. English
language—Rhetoric. I. Lehman, Jean.   II. Title.
PE1128.L494 1989
428.2'4—dc20

89-28037
CIP

Editorial/production supervision: Noël Vreeland Carter
Interior design: Ros Herion Freese
Cover design: Photo Plus Art
Manufacturing buyer: Ray Keating

We gratefully acknowledge the following publishers and companies for permission to reprint copyrighted materials:

University of Michigan Press for an adaptation of the table of potential domestic energy resources. Copyright © by the University of Michigan 1979. All rights reserved.

Lucasfilm, Ltd. for the photograph from "Return of the Jedi," © Lucasfilm Ltd. (LFL) 1983. All rights reserved.

The Educational Testing Service and the Graduate Management Admission Council for material from *GMAT 1987-88 Bulletin of Information*. Reprinted by permission.

Prentice-Hall, Inc. for material from Charles Oliver, HOW TO TAKE STANDARDIZED TESTS, © 1981, p. 2. Reprinted by permission of Prentice-Hall, Inc., Englewood Cliffs, N.J.

Our thanks also to the following companies for providing photographs for use in this book:

MCI Telecommunications Corporation

Xerox Corporation

Cray Research, Inc.

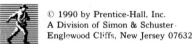

Prentice-Hall International (UK) Limited, *London*
Prentice-Hall of Australia Pty. Limited, *Sydney*
Prentice-Hall Canada Inc., *Toronto*
Prentice-Hall Hispanoamericana, S.A., *Mexico*
Prentice-Hall of India Private Limited, *New Delhi*
Prentice-Hall of Japan, Inc., *Tokyo*
Simon & Schuster Asia Pte. Ltd., *Singapore*
Editora Prentice-Hall do Brasil, Ltda , *Rio de Janeiro*

Introduction

Visions: An Academic Writing Text is part of a series of writing books for college/ university or adult students of English as a Second Language. It integrates writing skills for academic purposes. This book is coordinated with *Visions: A Pre-Intermediate Grammar* but can be used independently.

Subtechnical vocabulary, vocabulary common across academic and technical fields, is introduced through exercises in which students discover meaning through context. This subtechnical vocabulary is usually more difficult for students than are the technical terminologies of their individual fields; therefore, it is emphasized due to its importance to all college/university ESL students, regardless of their major fields. Content vocabulary exercises prepare students for the topic of the chapter. The vocabulary is then integrated in a reading whose topic is related to that of the main textbook chapter. Follow-up exercises emphasize general comprehension, vocabulary skills, sentence comprehension, paragraph organization, and discourse analysis. The grammar and/or discourse grammar in the reading is summarized and practiced.

Finally, students produce their own writing, guided by warm-up activities, brainstorming activities, guidelines for paragraph organization, and topical assignments that allow the use of vocabulary as well as sentence and discourse level grammar from the chapter. Using a process approach, students edit each other's writing. Checklists guide both the writing process and peer editing of drafts.

This book is intended for the low-intermediate level student who already has a knowledge of elementary English forms. It contains sufficient material for five class hours per week in an intensive semester course.

Acknowledgments

Our thanks to those friends and colleagues whose thoughts and ideas helped to shape this book: Elaine Galloway, Sarah Knotts, Carol Lindseth, Paul Martin, Christy Ott, Jim Ramsay, Rob Ruttan, Barbara Sihombing, Jean Sims, and Maria Thomas-Ružíc. We owe thanks also to the reviewers of the book and to Brenda White, Anne Riddick, Noël Vreeland Carter, and Ros Herion Freese for their invaluable advice and editorial assistance. Most of all, we thank our students through the years. Our experience with them helped us to formulate the techniques and methodology on which these materials are based. We would be pleased to hear from students and teachers using this book.

EL/JPL

To The Teacher

This *Academic Writing Text* is coordinated with and expands on the content in the main textbook, *Visions: A Pre-Intermediate Grammar*. It can be used with the main text or independently. The focus is on the integration of written skills for academic purposes: acquiring vocabulary from context, reading, understanding elements of grammar as they apply to discourse, and writing. This book is intended for use in the writing component of intensive English language programs.

Chapters begin with vocabulary discovery exercises. "Vocabulary in Context" includes both subtechnical and content vocabulary exercises. Subtechnical vocabulary consists of items common across academic and technical fields. These terms are reentered in later chapters as review. Content vocabulary is based on the topic of the "Reading," which is an extension of the topic in the corresponding main textbook chapter. All vocabulary exercises focus on the more difficult words in the reading. "Vocabulary in Context" can be assigned as homework and then discussed or done entirely in class. Students work without dictionaries on these exercises to develop the skill of guessing meaning from context. In later chapters, as students progress in their ability to guess meaning from context, vocabulary follow-up exercises check comprehension after the reading.

The "Reading" section begins with warm-up activities to direct attention to the content of the reading and/or to practice reading skills (predicting content, skimming, scanning). The reading can be covered in a variety of ways. To save class time, students can prepare before class by studying the reading. Class discussion can then center on their questions. Since the readings are short, students could also read them in class. Variations are reading parts of the material aloud to students, having students scan for specific details or skim for main ideas, and timed readings for comprehension.

"Understanding Through Writing" consists of explanation and exercises in General Comprehension, Word Study, Sentence Study, and Discourse Study. Students answer questions to gain a general understanding of the ideas; then they analyze the reading in terms of its vocabulary, sentences, and discourse. Skills covered include identifying true and false statements, answering questions, finding main ideas, identifying general and specific information, identifying synonymous sentences, making inferences, paraphrasing, identifying noun phrase and other referents, and so on. Students work on this section either in class or at home. The teacher checks comprehension with follow-up discussions.

"Getting Ready to Write Paragraphs" explores elements of discourse grammar from the reading. These points expand on the grammar presented in the corresponding chapter of the main text and have been selected on the basis of their frequency in written discourse rather than in conversation. Explanation can be discussed in class; associated exercises can be assigned as homework. In Recognition Exercises, students first identify and then write original sentences using the grammatical elements. Additional sentence-level exercises provide more practice of the material.

The answer key is for those exercises in the first part of each chapter only. It is made available for self-study or in-class use.

In the final section, "Writing Paragraphs," students apply what they have learned throughout the chapter. Using a process approach to writing, students brainstorm for ideas, organize, write, and revise two or more drafts. A variety of topic ideas that center around the content of the chapter are suggested. Students are also encouraged to generate their own ideas as topics. In some of the later chapters, students write compositions. Many of the paragraph topics throughout the book can be adapted for longer pieces of writing.

More class time is necessary for "Writing Paragraphs" than for other sections. Explanatory material is discussed; then students explore topics and generate ideas by brainstorming. Brainstorming activities alleviate the first, often nerve-wracking phase of writing when the student has decided on a topic but has nothing on paper. Students concentrate on writing words and phrases, making a list, or drawing a diagram. The product is not important at this point; students will have something on paper to work from or at least to think about. Various techniques for brainstorming are explored since different strategies work for different writers.

An explicit demonstration of brainstorming technique is helpful to students, many of whom are not familiar with what it is or why they are doing it. To demonstrate, the teacher might select transportation, the classification topic that students will work with in Chapter One. The teacher writes the topic on the board along with one related word or phrase, say *hydrofoil* or *space shuttle*. Students are invited to write one or two words each on the board. When everyone has contributed something, there will be a variety of ideas related to transportation on the board. Students then put the words in groups of their own choosing on a piece of paper. After several minutes, they compare their classifications in pairs. Finally, a few share their divisions with the class. This kind of introductory activity shows students the creative potential of a brainstorming activity, helps them to see that not every idea may be relevant, and gets them working with and learning from each other from the outset. Such an activity provides a transition to later chapters where students are expected to work in pairs on brainstorming.

After generating and organizing their ideas, students are encouraged to do the actual writing in class also. Students check each other's work and discuss it. Peer discussion and editing are valuable tools in revision. Revision can be started in class and completed as homework. A checklist gives students task-based suggestions on how to check their own and others' work for revision. Students consult the checklist before and after writing.

Throughout the writing process, students gain from the insights of other class members. They work together during brainstorming and again at the completion of successive stages: topic sentence, organizational notes, first and second drafts. For brainstorming, the work is creative and freewheeling. Students' later discussion about revision is structured by the items on the checklist. Before any kind of pair or group work begins, however, students need to be clear on what they are to accomplish. The teacher then selects students to work together or can let students decide on partners. Cooperative learning encourages students to exchange information and ideas. It also serves to solidify and integrate all four language skills: listening, speaking, reading, and writing.

To keep feedback and correction manageable, teachers often work with only a few types of errors. Many writing teachers react only to content and organization the first time a paper is turned in and then focus on grammar and mechanics in revised papers. With regard to content, focus might center on support of topic or thesis statement, for example. As for form, attention to verb forms, sequence signals, or any emphasis of the current chapter is appropriate. The checklist is another way to limit content suggestions and corrections. After the teacher comments on students' work, they are encouraged to revise and resubmit it. Like professional writers, they will discover more about what they want to say in successive drafts.

Following is one possible lesson plan for Chapter One. No textbook can substitute for the interest, vitality, and up-to-date knowledge that a teacher brings to class. Likewise, teachers are the best judge of how to pace and modify chapters to accommodate the interests and abilities of their students.

CHAPTER ONE LESSON PLAN

	Day 1	Day 2	Day 3
Review		Go over General Comp. Answer questions on Reading.	Collect Exercise 3.
New Material	Parts 1 & 2: Vocabulary, Warm-Up, & Reading	Part 4: Capitalization & Punctuation, Exercise 1. Joining Ideas & Exercise 2	Part 5: Prefixes Exercises 4, 5, & 6. Part 6: Warm-Up
Homework	Part 3: General Comp.	Exercise 3 to turn in.	Read Paragraphs of Classification

	Day 4	Day 5	Day 6
Review	Groups discuss Paragraphs of Classification	Discuss diagrams in pairs.	Go over Editing the First Draft; review Checklist.
New Material	Demonstration of brainstorming technique, Getting Started, Writing a Topic Sentence	Go over Writing a First Draft & Checklist. Students write first drafts.	Students edit their own work, trade papers, edit each other's work, & discuss.
Homework	Read Getting Organized. Draw a diagram.	Read Editing the First Draft.	Revise paragraphs to turn in.

Contents

Chapter Six: Solar Energy   72

Part 1: Vocabulary in Context

Subtechnical Vocabulary
Word Opposites

Part 2: Reading: Home Heating: Solar Energy

Warm-Up Activity: Skimming

Part 3: Understanding Through Writing

General Comprehension
Word Study
Sentence Study: Identifying Synonymous Sentences
Discourse Study: Sentence Reference

Part 4: Getting Ready to Write Paragraphs

The Present Tense
Recognition Exercise
Exercise 1
Exercise 2

Part 5: Writing Paragraphs

Warm-Up Activities: Paragraph Writing Guidelines, Description of a Process
Choosing a Topic: Description of a Process
Brainstorming for Ideas: Listing Steps in a Process
Writing a First Draft
Checklist
Revising the First Draft

Chapter Seven: Law   86

Part 1: Vocabulary in Context

Content Vocabulary: Law
Subtechnical Vocabulary: Parts of Speech

Part 2: Reading: American Telephone and Telegraph: A Regulated Monopoly?

Warm-Up Activity: Scanning

Part 3: Understanding Through Writing

General Comprehension: Finding the Main Idea
Word Study
Discourse Study: Reference to People and Things, Time and Place
Exercise 1

Part 2: Reading: Banking in the United States

Warm-Up Activity: Skimming

Part 3: Vocabulary Follow-Up

Subtechnical Vocabulary

Part 4: Understanding Through Writing

General Comprehension
Sentence Study: Paraphrasing
   Exercise 1
Discourse Study: *One(s)/the One(s)* for Reference
   Exercise 2

Part 5: Getting Ready To Write Paragraphs

Conjunctions: *Yet* and *Nor*
Giving Advice
   Recognition Exercise
   Exercise 3
   Exercise 4
   Exercise 5

Part 6: Writing Paragraphs

Warm-Up Activity
Getting Started: Description of a Process
Writing a First Draft
Checklist
Revising the First Draft

Chapter Eleven: Special Effects in the Movies   *141*

Part 1: Reading: Movies with Special Effects

Warm-Up Activity: Discussion Questions

Part 2: Vocabulary Follow-Up

Content Vocabulary: Special Effects

Part 3: Understanding Through Writing

General Comprehension: Inferences
Word Study
Sentence Study: Paraphrasing
Discourse Study: Using Synonyms

Writing the First Draft
Checklist
Revising the First Draft

CHAPTER ONE

Education

Educational programs can have different purposes. Two types of educational programs after the high-school level are academic and vocational.

Part 1
Vocabulary in Context

When a new word is *in context*, the words in the sentences around the new word tell you its meaning. Practice guessing the meanings of words in context. You will see these words again in the reading for this chapter.

Content Vocabulary: Education

Answer these questions.

1. Advanced Grammar and Beginning Writing are **courses** in an English language school. General Biology is a **course** in science at a college.

   Give an example of a **course** in mathematics. _____

2. A medical student has a 4-year **program**. The school tells him or her the courses to take. The student has a plan of the courses for all 4 years.

   a. Is a **program** a plan? _____ *yes* _____

   b. Is a **program** a class? _____ *no* _____

3. An **undergraduate** student has a general education program with many different courses. After this, a student can study in a **graduate** program. A **graduate** student takes courses in one subject.

   Write **graduate** or **undergraduate** under these schedules:

Jack		Janet	
9:00	English Composition	9:00	Non-Euclidean Geometry
11:00	History	11:00	Differential Equations IV
1:00-3:00	Biology Lab	1:00	Advanced Boulean Algebra

4. After a 4-year undergraduate program, a student gets a **bachelor's degree**. After a 1- or 2-year graduate program, a student has a **master's degree**. After a graduate program of 4 to 7 years, a student gets a **doctoral degree (a doctorate)**.

   a. In 3, for what **degree** is Jack working? _bachelor's_

   b. What degree will Janet get after 6 years? _doctoral_

5. A **university** is for undergraduate and graduate education. Students can get three types of degrees: bachelor's, master's, and doctoral. A **college** is usually for undergraduates and gives the bachelor's only.

   Write the names of a **college** and a **university** in the United States.

   _____   _____

6. Janet wants to teach math. She is in an **academic** program. Her brother wants to repair computers. He is at a **vocational** school.

   Write *A* for the **academic** programs and *V* for the **vocational** programs:

   _A_ English literature   _A_ Architecture   _V_ TV repair

   _V_ Food service   _V_ Carpentry   _A_ Art history

   _A_ Chemistry   _A_ Secretarial skills   _A_ Biology

Subtechnical Vocabulary

Every field of study has special words, or technical vocabulary. **Subtechnical** vocabulary is the vocabulary of academic English. We use it in all fields of study. These words are from the reading in this chapter.

Circle a or b.

Example: After secondary school, **post-**secondary education is usual for good students.

   Post- means: a. after
   b. school

1. I have three sports **skills.** I can play tennis, baseball, and football. I did well in all three sports in high school.

   A **skill** is: a. a game like tennis or baseball
   b. something a person can do well

2. Jack has a **full** bottle of cola. It's a hot day. Jack drinks half of the bottle fast. Now it is only half-**full**.

   Which is the **full** bottle?   a.   b.

3. It is **common** for French or Spanish speakers to say in English, "I have 20 years." They mean, "I am 20 years old." This is a usual

mistake for beginning students of English. They make this mistake a
lot.

Common means: a. usual
                       b. beginning

4. The **reason** for this mistake is that students are translating from
their languages to English. That is why they make the mistake in
English.

A **reason** tells: a. where
                      b. why

5. To go to a different country, you need a
visa. There are many **types** of visas for
the United States. One **type** is a student
visa for people with I-20s from U.S.
schools. Other kinds are tourist and
worker visas.

A **type** is: a. a visa
             b. a kind

6. Last year Statewide University had
15,000 students. This year it added a
nursing school, and now there are 15,320
students. This is an **increase** of 320
students.

An **increase** is: a. a higher number
                 b. a lower number

7. "I'm tired of studying. Do you want to see a movie?"
"I'd like to. It's a **possibility,** but I need to call my sister first. I'll
call you back after I talk to her."

A **possibility** is: a. something that is not possible
                     b. something that is possible

Part 2
Reading

Warm-up Activities: Discussion, Predicting Content

A. A career is a profession or occupation for which you study. A career
is a person's lifework. Teaching is an example of a career. What are
some other careers? For what career are you studying?

B. Looking at only the first sentence of each paragraph will give you a
general idea of a reading. When you have a general idea, it is easier
to understand the specifics. Read the first sentence in each paragraph of the reading. Then answer these questions about the topic.

1. What is the general topic of the reading? _the types of ed. f_

2. Put a check (✓) next to the things you will probably learn more about when you look at the entire reading:

   _____ university degree programs around the world

   _✓_ university degree programs in the United States

   _____ high-school education

   _✓_ academic programs and degrees

   _____ the cost of a university education in the United States

   Return to this section after you read. How well did you guess?

POST-SECONDARY EDUCATION IN THE UNITED STATES

1   Forty-five percent of the 18- to 19-year-olds in the United States are students in post-secondary educational programs. About 22% of the 20- to 24-year-olds are full-time or part-time students. A lot of these students are in two common types of post-secondary programs: academic and vocational programs.

2   In general, universities have two types of academic programs: undergraduate and graduate. Undergraduate students take general courses. They decide on a major in their first or second year and study this subject for the last 2 or 3 years. Common undergraduate degrees are the Bachelor of Science (B.S.), the Bachelor of Arts (B.A), and the Bachelor in Business Administration (B.B.A.). Some undergraduates continue in graduate programs. As graduate students, they study one subject only. Master's programs are usually 2 years long. Typical graduate degrees are the Master of Arts (M.A.), the Master of Science (M.S.), the Master of Business Administration (M.B.A.), and the Master of Engineering (M.Eng.). Students who continue after a master's program are working for the Doctor of Philosophy (Ph.D. or doctorate). A Ph.D. usually takes about 6 years. For a student with an undergraduate degree, a second possibility is a professional graduate program. Medical schools and law schools are examples. The degrees are the Doctor of Medicine (M.D.) and the Doctor of Jurisprudence (J.D.). A student works 4 years for an M.D. and 3 years to be a lawyer.

3   In the United States, the number of students working for academic degrees is not on the increase. One reason is an increase in the number of students in a second type of post-secondary program: vocational education. Vocational programs teach technical and manual skills to high-school graduates. TV electronics is one example of a

technical skill. There are also manual skills such as woodworking. After a year or two, a student can use the skill at work. The possibility of a job in the near future interests people in vocational education.

4   The main reason people go to school is to get good jobs. Many careers are not open to people without high-school diplomas. The door to career possibilities opens further for students with college and vocational degrees. University graduates are often the leaders in education, business, government, and industry.

Part ❸
Understanding Through Writing

General Comprehension

A paragraph is a group of sentences that all discuss one main idea. When writers begin a new idea, they begin a new paragraph. How many paragraphs are there in the reading for this chapter?

Fill in the blanks with words from paragraphs 2 and 3 of the reading.

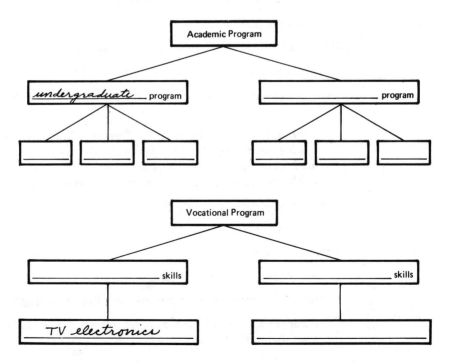

Part 4
Getting Ready to Write Paragraphs

Capitalization

Use capital letters for:

names:	**G**eorge, **D**eborah, **T**erry, **S**mith
titles:	**M**rs. Duncan, **M**r. Davis, **P**rof. Dresden, **D**r. Moore
streets:	**W**estern **A**venue, **Q**ueen **S**treet, **G**lebe **P**oint **R**oad
cities:	**T**okyo, **L**os **A**ngeles, **J**akarta, **S**eoul
states and provinces:	**N**ew **Y**ork, **O**regon, **T**exas, **B**ritish **C**olumbia
countries:	**K**uwait, **F**rance, the **U**nited **S**tates, **C**hina
geographical features:	**M**ount **E**verest, the **Y**angtze **R**iver, the **I**ndian **O**cean
schools:	the **U**niversity of **C**alifornia, **T**ulane **U**niversity
abbreviations:	**UCLA, NASA, CBS, FBI, NYSE**

Use capitals also for the word *I* and for the first word in every sentence:

The applications are here. **M**y friend and **I** will apply to four schools.

Punctuation

Use a period (.) at the end of statements:

I want to go to Cornell**.**

Use a question mark (?) at the end of questions:

Are you interested in Cornell or Stanford**?**

Use a comma (,) between items in a list. The last item has a comma + *and:*

I will apply to San Diego State**,** Stanford**,** Cal Poly**, and** Cornell.
I will need an application**,** a financial statement**,** a health statement**, and** an application fee for each school.
I will read catalogs**,** fill out applications**,** send them off**, and** wait.

Use an apostrophe (') in short forms:

I**'**m, you**'**re, she**'**s

and in possessives:

the woman**'**s, someone**'**s, Jack**'**s.

Punctuation always comes at the end of a line of writing:

I will work hard. I**'**ll read catalogs, fill out applications**,**
send them off, and wait.

NOT:

> I will work hard. I'll read catalogs, fill out applications
> , send them off, and wait.

EXERCISE 1

Add capital letters and punctuation to these paragraphs. The first one is an example.

today i m going to talk about how to choose a college or university there are many schools in this country it's hard to decide which ones are best for you i had the same problem twenty years ago

the first thing to think about is getting information about schools your college library has a lot of college catalogs they give important information about each school: programs courses applications and housing look at several catalogs for the area you're interested in i wanted to be in southern california, so i applied to ucla ucsd usc and the university of redlands look first at the schools in your favorite city you will have a good idea of the programs at the schools after you read some catalogs

another way to get information about schools is to talk to an advisor and to students in your major field of study it's a good idea to visit the schools see the campuses talk to an advisor and then decide

Joining Ideas: *And, Also*

And and *also* introduce additional information. Use *and* to join two subjects, verbs, adjectives, places, etc.:

> A master's **and** a doctorate are graduate degrees.
> Graduate students **read and write** a lot more than undergraduates.
> Graduate programs are usually **long and difficult.**
> Students spend a lot of time **at their desks and in the library.**

Use a comma + *and* to join two sentences with similar information:

> I have a master's degree. + My brother has a Ph.D. =
> I have a master's degree, **and** my brother has a Ph.D.

Use *also* to join the ideas in two separate sentences:

> My brother has a B.S. He **also** has a Ph.D.
>   (also = in addition to his B.S.)
> Janet studies on Sundays. She **also** plays tennis in the afternoons.
>   (also = in addition to studying)

EXERCISE 2

*Fill in nouns from the reading and **be**. Use commas + **and** for lists.*

Example: <u>The M.D. and the J.D. are</u> two professional graduate degrees.
(be)

1. _____

   _____ _____ two post-secondary programs.
   (be)

2. _____

   _____
   (be)

   three examples of undergraduate degrees.

3. Three examples of graduate degrees <u>are</u> <u>B.A, M.A and M.D.</u>
   (be)

   _____

4. _____ _____
   (be)

   two examples of vocational skills.

EXERCISE 3

*Read this paragraph. Then rewrite it on a separate piece of paper. Use **and** to join phrases and sentences. Use **also** to join ideas in separate sentences. Use commas + **and** for lists.*

There are several types of technical education in Newcountry. Students can study engineering. They can study computer science. They can study telecommunications. These are the fields of study that Newcountry needs most. These are the fields of study that Newcountry's economy needs most. Students can study many types of engineering. The country needs transportation engineers. The country needs electronics engineers. In the area of computer science, students can study software production. They can study applications of computers in business. Telecommunications is very important in business. Telecommunications is important in government. It is a career for the present. It is a career for the future. The young people of Newcountry are working hard to prepare themselves for many careers of the future.

Example: <u>There are several types of technical education in Newcountry.</u>
<u>Students can study engineering, computer science, and</u>
<u>telecommunications.</u>

Part 5
Using Prefixes

MAN: I have a lot of free time, and I want to go back to college. But a sixty-year-old undergraduate is **unusual**, right?

ADVISOR: Well, yes. It is **uncommon** for people your age to go back to school. But that doesn't mean it's **impossible**.

Sixty-year-old undergraduates are **not** common. =
Sixty-year-old undergraduates are **un**common.

Un- is a prefix, an addition at the beginning of a word. It changes the meaning of the word. *Un-* makes words negative:

Is biology interesting or **uninteresting** to you?

Other negative prefixes are *non-*, *im-*, and *in-*:

Is the man's idea **impossible**? Is it **inappropriate**?

unlikely	noninstructional	improbable	incomplete
unkind	nonacademic	imperfect	inappropriate

EXERCISE 4

Decide if each statement is true or false. Mark T or F in the blanks.

1. __F__ A vocational program is a nonacademic program.

2. __T__ A person who is sick all the time is unhealthy.

3. __F__ Life is generally uninteresting.

4. __F__ You are a non-native speaker of English.

5. __F__ Answers 1–4 in this exercise are incorrect.

6. __F__ The United States is an inexpensive country to live in.

7. __F__ In general, scientists are unintelligent.

EXERCISE 5

Circle the one word that does not mean the same as the other words.

Example: unusual, different, unordinary, (ordinary)

1. nonacademic, (vocational,) nonvocational

2. uninteresting, boring, (interesting)

3. incorrect, (correct,) wrong, not right

4. cheap, (expensive,) inexpensive

5. intelligent, bright, ~~unintelligent,~~ smart

6. untypical, ~~common,~~ uncommon, unusual

7. unhealthy, sick, ~~healthy~~

8. impossible, not possible, ~~possible~~

EXERCISE 6

Discuss these questions in small groups.

1. Is it appropriate here to snap your fingers for the waiter's attention? What is appropriate in your country?
2. Name a non-native speaker of English who speaks English very well.
3. What was a recent noninstructional event at your school? Did you go?
4. Do you think it is probable or improbable that one of your classmates will be an important political leader in his or her country?
5. What is common here but uncommon in your country?
6. What is one imperfect thing in the city where you are living?
7. What do you think is unlikely for the future?
8. Do you have any unusual interests or abilities?

Part 6
Writing Paragraphs

Warm-Up Activity: Classification

When we classify things, we put them into groups. We can classify *students* as graduates and undergraduates, for example:

level of education _____ (principle of classification)

graduate students _____ (type)

undergraduate students _____ (type)

For this classification, students are divided into groups by their level of education. This is the principle of classification.

What other classifications of students are possible? Decide first how to divide (a principle of classification). Then think of two or three groups or types. Discuss your classifications in pairs.

_____ (principle of classification)

_____ (type)

_____ (type)

_____ (type)

_____ (principle of classification)

_____ (type)

_____ (type)

_____ (type)

Paragraphs of Classification

In this section you will write paragraphs of classification.

Study these pictures, which show different kinds of communication. Then read the paragraph; notice how it follows the same organization as the pictures.

INSTRUMENTS OF COMMUNICATION

In today's busy world, three kinds of communication instruments are important. The telephone and tape recorder are examples of one type. With these instruments, people use sound to communicate. A second type of communication is mail. People use the written word to communicate by mail. Letters and magazines are examples. Mail is not as fast as other types of communication, but sometimes speed is not important. A more recent kind of communication is the computer. Communication with computers is fast and easy. People send electronic mail, or "E mail," to each other with computers. Millions of people use all three kinds of communication every day.

In small groups, discuss these questions about the paragraph.

1. Find the general sentence that tells what the writer will do in the paragraph. (This is the topic sentence.)

2. Find three sentences that introduce each type of communication. Do any of these sentences also give examples?

3. After each type of communication is introduced, at least one or two more sentences give specific information. Which of the three types of communication has the most discussion?

4. The last sentence gives a general idea again. It finishes the paragraph by mentioning the topic but saying something a little different about it. Another possibility is to restate the main idea in different words. A third possibility is to give an opinion.

Make up a different sentence of conclusion for this paragraph. Restate the main idea or give an opinion.

Getting Started

Use transportation as the topic to write a paragraph of classification. Begin by thinking about types of transportation and examples of each type. This picture shows city owned, privately owned, and corporate owned forms of transportation. What are other examples of each type?

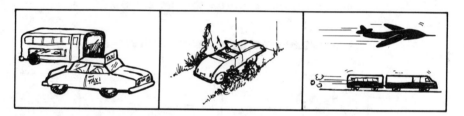

Writing a Topic Sentence

Write one general sentence about your topic. Do not write sentences like: *This paragraph is about ...., I am writing about a classification of ....* Instead, work on an interesting idea about the topic: types of transportation in large cities or in your capital city, transportation long ago, transportation today, rapid forms of transportation, etc.

In the 1900s, there were several effective forms of transportation. Transportation in (capital city) falls into three main categories.

Getting Organized

One way to organize ideas for writing is to draw a picture or diagram. The diagram in "General Comprehension," page 5, gives one idea of how to do this. It shows the content of paragraphs 2 and 3 of the reading. Your diagram can be anything that helps you.

Here is another diagram of paragraph 2 only with more detail. What are the main categories (types)? What are the examples?

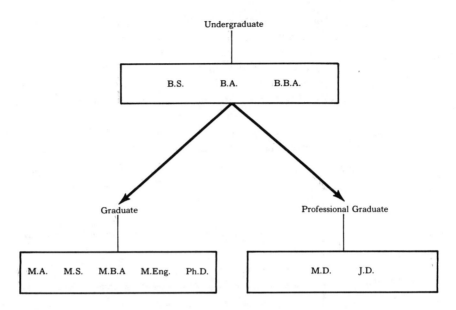

Academic Programs

Undergraduate

B.S.   B.A.   B.B.A.

Graduate   Professional Graduate

M.A.   M.S.   M.B.A   M.Eng.   Ph.D.   M.D.   J.D.

Draw a diagram for your paragraph on types of transportation, and fill in your types and examples. Write your topic sentence on this paper also.

Exchange papers with a partner. Study your partner's diagram carefully. Do you agree with the types and examples? Be sure to look at the topic sentence. Does it introduce the classification? Is it clear to you? Is it interesting? Ask any questions you have. Make any suggestions you can.

Writing a First Draft

Write your ideas in paragraph form. For your first draft, do not worry about spelling and punctuation. Leave these things for later. The most important thing is to get your ideas on paper. It is helpful to skip lines so that there is room to make changes

Begin the paragraph with your topic sentence. Then use your diagram to introduce each category and some examples of it. (See Exercise 2 on page 8 for sentences that introduce examples.) Write something about each type. Discuss the size or importance, or explain more about it. Write a concluding sentence at the end. Restate your topic sentence or give an opinion.

Editing the First Draft

Read over your paper carefully using the following checklist. You may have a lot of changes you want to make. Good writers almost always write a first draft and then reread and rewrite several times before deciding on the sentences they want.

Checklist

1. Find a clear statement of the topic of the paragraph.
2. Find clear statements introducing the categories or types.
3. Find two or more examples of each type.
4. Find places where there is discussion of each type. Which is the most interesting discussion section? Why?
5. Read the paragraph again. Are there a lot of short sentences? Can you join some sentences with *and*, or join ideas with *also*?
6. Read the paper two more times. The first time, check spelling. The second time, check punctuation. Are there commas for lists of items?

After you use the checklist, your edited paper might look like this:

> ~~The government of (Country) has training~~ Certain
> ~~programs for several important~~ are the most important for the development of (Country) kinds of
> technical education. ~~In this paragraph I will~~
> ~~make a classification of the types of~~
> ~~technical education.~~ The ~~government~~ country ~~wants~~ needs
> more engineers ~~for~~ in electronics and
> transportation. (Country) is developing quickly~~,~~
> ~~we~~ and we need more transportation engineers to
> ~~desing~~ design roads and bridges. Electronics is
> economically
> also important~~,~~ because we export a lot.
> also benefits from
> The government ~~has~~ computer science and
> telecommunications training. These programs
> government-funded
> are available at the university, but the
> private
> best programs are at technical schools.
> ~~When we go to the~~ In the 21st century, these skills
> are the most important for my country~~,~~
> ~~my area of the world~~ and the world economy.

In the edited paragraph example, what is the first topic sentence? What is the difference in the new topic sentence?

When you finish making changes on your paragraph, copy it over and exchange papers with your partner. Look at your partner's paper carefully. Ask about anything that is not clear to you. Use the checklist to go over the paragraph. Underline any part of the paragraph that you have a question about. Then discuss both paragraphs together.

Revising the First Draft

Rewrite your paragraph to hand in. Remember your partner's questions and suggestions.

CHAPTER TWO

Invention: The Telephone

The invention of the telephone was the result of ideas from a number of different countries. It began in the United States with Alexander Graham Bell and was improved with the ideas of inventors from around the world.

Part ❶
Vocabulary in Context

Content Vocabulary: Invention

A. *Read this story.*

1   Roderic Mason is an **inventor**. His head is full of **ideas** about new machines, new instruments—things to make life easy. Today his **idea** is an **improvement** on the bicycle. The bicycle is slow. It is hard work going uphill. In Roderic's mind is a picture of a better bicycle. He **imagines** it with pleasure. It is fast, and no work is necessary to ride it. The **equipment** is simple: an electric battery and a small machine to make the wheels go around.

2   Roderic uses his skill as an **inventor** to make the small machine. Then he puts the **equipment** on the bicycle. He works hard all week. Finally he is finished. The **result** of his work is an electric bicycle.

3   After a while, Roderic is unhappy. The only person who likes his invention is his mother. Many people ride bicycles for exercise and are not interested in an electric bicycle.

B. *Answer questions about the story. Then choose definitions. Write letters in the blanks.*

  a. a thought, a plan
  b. something that comes from an action or actions; the outcome
  c. things that are used together to make or do something
  d. an increase in the usefulness; something that is better
✓ e. a person who thinks of and makes improvements
  f. to make a picture in the mind

Example: Write the sentence in paragraph 1 that tells what is in an **inventor's** head.

His head is full of new ideas about machines, new instru-
ments—things to make life easy.

Inventor means __e__.

1. Roderic's mind is full of **ideas**. What is his **idea** today?
   His idea today is an improvement on the bicycle.
   Idea means __a__.

2. Roderic's invention is an **improvement** on the bicycle. Write two sentences from paragraph 1 about the bicycle before the **improvement**.
   _____
   Improvement means __d__.

3. Roderic **imagines** his new bicycle with pleasure. Write the sentence from paragraph 1 that describes **imagining**.
   In Roderic's mind is a picture of better bicycle.
   Imagine means __f__.

4. What is the **equipment** for Roderic's invention?
   An electrical battery
   Equipment means __c__.

5. What is the **result** of Roderic's work?
   _____
   Result means __b__.

Subtechnical Vocabulary

A. *Underline words that help you to understand the words in* **boldface**.

Example: For me algebra is **simple**. It is <u>easy for me to understand.</u>

1. One inventor usually doesn't <u>make an invention alone</u>. Other inventors **help**. They <u>work with the first inventor.</u>
2. An inventor is <u>just one person</u>. Three inventors all working on one problem is a **group**.
3. Roderic is practicing a talk about the electric bicycle with his friends. After a few minutes, he asks, "Is it a boring talk?"
   "No, <u>don't stop; tell us more</u>," I say.
   "It's interesting. Please **continue**," his sister Angela agrees.

B. *Write short answers.*

1. **Communication** is giving and receiving information. Two types are writing and speaking. We use **instruments** to make **communication** easy and fast. A telephone is an **instrument** for spoken **communication**.

   a. What type of **communication** is easier for you in your first language, writing or speaking? _speaking_

   b. What type of **communication** is easier for you in English, listening or reading? _reading_

   c. Is a television an **instrument** of communication? _yes_

2. **Local** calls are to nearby places. A **local** call can be to a place in the same city or to a different town that is close.

   Give an example of a **local** call: from _Riverside_ to _Colton_.

3. Calls from Los Angeles to Honolulu are **long-distance** calls. There are many miles between the two cities. These calls can be expensive.

   a. Is the **distance** the place or the number of miles? _number of miles_

   b. Give an example of a **long-distance** call from your city:

      from _Riverside_ to _Mexico_.

4. Last month my bill had 10 long-distance calls. **Only** nine calls were correct. The tenth call was to Detroit, Michigan. I don't know anyone in Detroit. I paid for **only** nine calls.

   a. What does **only nine calls** mean, "nine calls but no more" or "nine calls or more"? _nine calls but no more_

   b. Do you have **only** one telephone or more than one telephone? _only one_

Part 2
Reading

Warm-Up Activity: Predicting Content

Pictures can help you to get a general idea of a reading. When you have a general idea, it is easier to understand what you read. Look at the pictures in the reading. Also think about these words you have studied: *inventor*, *improvement*, *equipment*, *communication*. What will you probably read about? Write one sentence about the general topic of the reading.

Now look at the first sentence in each paragraph of the reading. Reread your sentence. Change it if you want to. Then ask a partner to look at it. Discuss your different ideas about the topic.

1   Today the telephone is an instrument of international communication. It allows us to make calls all over the world. In 1876, telephone calls from Seattle to Singapore were unthinkable. Alexander Graham Bell had a simple telephone in 1876, but communication was not easy. The sound was weak, and the words were unclear. The telephone was for local calls only because the sound traveled only a few miles.

2   How did we get from the local lines of 1876 to the international lines of today? It was the result of work in different countries. Over the years, inventors from Germany, Italy, France, England, Denmark, Sweden, and the United States helped to improve the equipment. In England, two inventors, C.A. McEvoy and G.E. Pritchett, had an idea; soon the receiver and the transmitter were on only one piece of equipment. In Denmark, Carl Emil Krarup made an improvement in sound. As a result, sound was louder over a distance. We use his improvement in telephone lines under water.

3   Scientists and inventors all over the world continue to improve telecommunications because fast communication is important today. Computers communicate with computers over telephone lines, and satellites help us to communicate sound and pictures over great dis-

tances. Another invention is the telecopier, which sends copies over telephone lines in seconds. During a phone conversation, one person puts a paper into a telecopier; the second person receives an exact copy immediately.

4   In 1876, most people couldn't imagine an international call. The idea of communicating from one country to another by sound seemed impossible. Today both sound and pictures can travel thousands of miles in seconds. International students can call home easily, <u>thanks to an international group of inventors.</u>

Part 3
Understanding Through Writing

Word Study

Write words from the reading.

1. Which word in paragraph 1 tells you that international calls were impossible in 1876? ___unthinkable___

2. What are the words in the third sentence of paragraph 2 that mean "from 1876 to the present"? ___improve___

3. In paragraph 4, does *today* mean "this day" or "at present"? ___at present___

4. What words in paragraph 4 mean "because of"? ___thanks to___

Sentence Study: Giving Information

Write complete sentence answers.

Example: Who was the inventor of the telephone?

   Alexander Graham Bell was the inventor of the telephone.

1. In past years, inventors from many countries helped to improve telecommunications. What countries were they from?
   ___Germany, Italy, France, England, Denmark, and the U.S.___

2. Who were the two Englishmen? ___C.A. McEvoy and G.E Pritchett___

3. What was Krarup's occupation? _____

4. What are the three instruments of communication in paragraph 3?
   _____

Discourse Study: Paragraph Organization

Answer questions about organization.

1. English writing commonly begins with known information and then gives new or unknown information. General information is well known, and it usually comes before specific information:

   > International communication is quick and easy today. Direct dialing allows many international calls to get through in seconds.

   a. Which is more general: *international communication* or *direct dialing*?

   _____

   b. Which is more specific: *quick* or *in seconds*? _____

   c. Reread the first paragraph of the reading. Does it show typical English organization? (Does the first paragraph give general information?)

   _____

2. When writers give examples, they give specific information. In this reading, specific examples are in which paragraphs? (*Circle two choices.*)
   a. paragraph 1   b. paragraph 2   c. paragraph 3

3. After discussing the topic, writers will sometimes *extend* the topic: They will talk about something different but with important similarities. Which paragraph extends the topic? (*Circle one.*)
   a. paragraph 2   b. paragraph 3   c. paragraph 4

4. A title usually tells the topic. Which is the best title for this reading? (*Circle one.*)
   a. The Telephone Today
   b. The Telephone: An International Invention
   c. The Telephone: A Simple Invention of Alexander Graham Bell

Part 4
Getting Ready to Write Paragraphs

Using Place and Time Expressions

Place and time expressions can come at the end of the sentence:

> Roderic and his sister Angela were busy **in Baltimore**. They went to a meeting there **in November**.

or at the beginning:

> Roderic talks on the telephone a lot. **Yesterday** he was on the phone for 3 hours. **Today** he was on the phone from 10:00 to 11:15.

Roderic was on the phone a lot yesterday and today. The two sentences have **similar** information. Now look at these place expressions:

> Last month was good for spring vacationers. **In Florida** it was 80 degrees. Roderic got a postcard from a friend there and flew down to Florida. **In Colorado** it was 47 degrees. The Rocky Mountains were full of skiers. Angela loves to ski. She flew to Aspen for a long weekend.

The sentences with place expressions have **different** information. Place expressions at the beginning help to point out the differences. Places and times at the beginning can show similarities and differences.

Joining Sentences: *And, But*, the Semicolon, *Because*

Writing is interesting when we join some sentences. There are many ways to do this. Review the use of *and*. Study *but*, the semicolon (;), and *because*.

And: Similar Information

Angela and I are both professionals.

I am a teacher.		Angela is a lawyer.	(two sentences)
I am a teacher,	**and**	Angela is a lawyer.	(one sentence)
\‾‾clause‾‾/		\‾‾‾‾clause‾‾‾‾/	

And introduces similar information. The "sentences in a sentence" are called *clauses*. A clause always has a subject and a verb. A comma comes before *and* + clause.

But: Different Information

Angela and I walked 3 miles.

Angela was tired.		I was ready for 3 more miles.
Angela was tired,	**but**	I was ready for 3 more miles.
\‾‾clause‾‾/		\‾‾‾‾‾‾clause‾‾‾‾‾‾/

But introduces different information. A comma comes before *but* + clause.

The Semicolon: Related Information (Similar or Different)

Angela and I are both professionals.
I am a teacher; Angela is a lawyer. (similar)

Angela and I walked 3 miles.
Angela was tired; I was ready for 3 more miles. (different)

A semicolon (;) joins sentences. A comma (,) does not.

Because: Telling Reasons

The clause after *because* gives a reason. There is no comma:

Angela is a good lawyer **because** she works hard.

The electric bicycle was
    unpopular **because** people use bikes to exercise.

RECOGNITION EXERCISE

See the reading on page 19 to answer. Then discuss your answers in pairs.

1. Find the two sentences in paragraph 1 that begin with times. Is the information in the sentences similar or different?

2. Find the sentence in paragraph 1 with *and*. What is similar? (Is it two inventions, two problems, or two pieces of equipment?)

3. a. Find the sentence in paragraph 1 with *but*. Does this sentence show a similarity or a difference?

    b. Complete this sentence: I have a telephone, but _____ .

4. We use the semicolon (;) instead of *and* or *but*. It is not used often.

    a. Write the number of times you see semicolons in the reading. _____

    b. Do they mean *and* or *but* in the reading? _____

5. See the end of paragraph 1. Why was the telephone for local calls only in 1876? (*Write a complete sentence answer with two clauses.*)

EXERCISE 1

*Read the first sentence. On a separate piece of paper, complete the second sentence with comma + **and** + a or b.*

Example: Businesses usually have touch-tone phones.

Touch-tone phones are easy to use _____.
a. they are very fast
b. they are quite slow

Touch-tone phones are easy to use, and they are very fast.

1. Henry Ford invented the first popular car in the United States, the Model T.

   The Model T was much faster than horses *but it was a little dangerous.*

   a. it was fun and exciting
   b. it was a little dangerous

2. Lazio Biro of Argentina invented the ballpoint pen.

   The ballpoint pen makes writing easy *and it is popular all over the world.*

   a. it is popular all over the world
   b. it doesn't write as clearly as a fountain pen

3. Zacharias Janssen of the Netherlands invented the microscope.

   The microscope made very small things larger _____.

   a. scientists learned a lot using it
   b. scientists found it difficult to use

4. Benjamin Franklin invented the bifocal lens.

   The bifocal lens helped people to see things close to them, *and it helped them to see far away.*

   a. it cost too much for most people
   b. it helped them to see far away

5. Howard Aiken developed the first digital computer in 1944.

   The computer worked with a lot of information *but computers today are much faster.*

   a. computers today are much faster
   b. it worked quickly

EXERCISE 2

On a separate piece of paper, complete the second sentence with comma +
but *+ a or b*

Example: I have an old dial telephone.

It still works fine _____.

a. the color is an ugly green
b. the color is a pretty blue

It still works fine, but the color is an ugly green.

1. Telecopiers use telephone lines to send photocopies.

   Telecopiers are useful in large businesses _____.

   a. they are cheap to buy
   b. they are expensive to buy

2. A telephoto lens is used with a good camera.

   A telephoto lens increases the size of something far away _____.

   a. it isn't for close things
   b. it is helpful to the photographer

3. A teleprompter is a machine that shows a written speech line by line.

   The speaker can see the teleprompter _____.

   a. the audience can
   b. the audience can't

4. Inventors developed the first television during the 1920s.

   I like watching TV _____.

   a. the shows are great
   b. I don't like every show

5. Teleportation means moving someone a long distance by changing the body to energy.

   Teleportation is not possible today _____.

   a. it's unthinkable
   b. it's a possibility for the year 3000

EXERCISE 3

Write sentences about your country and a different country. Use place expressions and semicolons. Work on a separate piece of paper.

   Example: the money

   In Japan, the money is the yen; in Saudi Arabia, the money is the riyal.

1. the time now
2. a major university
3. a popular car
4. the national holiday
5. a popular pastime
6. a typical greeting

EXERCISE 4

A. *Use this information to write sentences about Elaine and Eileen. Use **and**. The first one is an example.*

> *SITUATION:* Elaine and Eileen were identical twins. As children they were alike in many ways. The similarities continued as they got older.

Elaine

a legal secretary
a golfer
in Chicago
the mother of five children
open and friendly

Eileen

a medical secretary
a tennis player
in Los Angeles
the mother of four children
funny and pleasant

As adults, Elaine and Eileen were alike in many ways. They were both secretaries. _Elaine was a legal secretary,_

and Eileen was a medical secretary.

They both liked outdoor sports. _Elaine liked golf, and_

_Eileen liked tennis_____ They both lived in big cities.

Elaine lived in Chicago, and Eileen lived in Los Angeles,

They both had large families. _Elaine had five children, and_

_Eileen had four Children_____ People liked both sisters.

_People liked Elaine, and Eileen too_____

In general, the twins had similar lives.

B. *On a piece of paper, write four or five sentences that tell how two members of your family are different. Use **but**.*

> *Example:* _I am tall, but my brother is medium-height._

EXERCISE 5

Answer in complete sentences on a piece of paper.

> *Example:* Why are you learning English?
>
> _I am learning English because I need it for work._

1. Why is English useful to you?
2. Why did you decide on English?
3. Why are you studying your major field?
4. Why is your major interesting to you?
5. Think of a recent event in the news. Tell why it happened. (*Write two or three sentences.*)

6. Think of a recent event in your country. Tell why it happened.

7. Who was recently elected in a country? Tell who, where, and why.

Part 5
Writing Paragraphs

Warm-Up Activity: Indenting Paragraphs

Read about paragraph form:

1   When writing a paragraph by hand, the writer *indents* the first line to show the paragraph beginning. In other words, the writer starts writing a few spaces in from the left margin. When typing or using a word processor, the writer can indent or use line spacing (a blank line between paragraphs). Line spacing also shows when one paragraph ends and when the next one begins.

2   There is actually little difference between typed and handwritten paragraphs. Typed work shows paragraph divisions by indenting from the left or by line spacing, but this is only a small difference in form. Writers should use one or the other throughout a paper.

3   *Using line spacing to show the beginning of a handwritten paragraph is not usual. Handwritten work shows paragraph beginnings by indenting four or five spaces from the left margin.*

4   When writing a paragraph, one thing to remember is that every line is filled up as much as possible to the right margin.
It is not correct form to leave space at the end of a line even if you finish a sentence.
The next sentence starts on the same line, not a new one.

Of these four paragraphs, which ones have correct form? _____

Main Idea, Topic Sentence, Paragraph Form

A paragraph has only one main idea. The main idea is in a topic sentence, the most general sentence in the paragraph. A topic sentence tells the topic and what the writer will say about it (the main idea).

See the paragraph about Elaine and Eileen in Exercise 4. The first sentence is the topic sentence. It tells the reader to look for similarities between the two women as adults. The other sentences give specific examples of similarities. The last sentence gives the main idea again, but in different words. This paragraph is typical:

Introduction: one or two general sentences about the topic and main idea

Discussion: three to eight sentences of specific examples or discussion

Conclusion: one or two sentences restating the main idea

Expository Writing

To explain is to make clear or understandable. In academic writing, it is common to tell about or explain something. This is called *expository* writing. Expository writing is not personal writing, so writers seldom use *I*. In expository writing, the focus is on the ideas, not the writer. Remember this when you work on a paragraph of explanation.

Deciding on a Topic: Paragraphs of Explanation

Think first about an invention (or discovery) that is interesting to you. See Exercises 1 and 2 for some ideas. Choose something that you know a little about already. You can choose something that is useful to your business or to your country, or something that is common, unusual, typical in (*country*), etc. The fact that the invention is useful in your business or typical in (*country*) can be the main idea of the paragraph.

Brainstorming for Ideas: Discussion Homework

Think about answers to these questions. Work alone.

Why is the invention special or interesting?
Do you know who invented it or where it was invented?
Why do people use the invention? What does it do? How is it helpful?
Is the invention something that everyone can use?
Is it a recent invention? Is it available today in most places?
What did people use instead of this invention 50 years ago?
What else can you say about it? Can you think of any improvements?

In pairs, discuss the questions for your topics. (You will probably write about only one or two questions.) Your partner will also ask you questions. This discussion will help you to think of more ideas.

Think about what you want to say in the paragraph. Make a list of ideas. Use an almanac or encyclopedia to learn who developed the invention and where, when, and why it was developed.

Writing a Topic Sentence

Write a topic sentence for the paragraph. You can write about the importance, popularity, or usefulness of the invention:

> In today's world, a photocopy machine is a necessary piece of equipment for both small and large businesses.

> Intensive farming is an especially important method in countries with small land areas.

> Christian Schönbein of Germany discovered ozone in 1839, but people are only beginning to understand its importance today.

Show your topic sentence and notes to a partner for discussion. Ask your partner to tell you if all the ideas fit your topic.

Writing a First Draft

Write down your ideas in sentences. Do not worry now about spelling or grammar. You can think about those things later. The most important thing is to get your ideas on paper.

When you finish, read your paragraph. What is the main idea? Do all the sentences discuss this main idea?

Use the following checklist. Make the changes you want to, and copy the paragraph over.

Exchange papers with your partner. Ask your partner to tell you about anything that is not clear. Use the checklist to go over your partner's work. Underline any sentences you have question about. Discuss both paragraphs using the checklist.

Checklist

1. What do you like best about this paragraph? Why?
2. Find a clear statement of the main idea of the paragraph.
3. Which sentences, if any, do not discuss the main idea?
4. Which sentences, if any, are unclear?
5. What do you want to learn more about? Where does the writer need more explanation?
6. Where can the writer use *and*, *but*, or *because* to join sentences?
7. Check paragraph form. Is the paragraph indented? Are lines filled to the right margin?
8. Reread the paragraph for spelling and punctuation.

Revising the First Draft

Think about what your partner said. Work especially with any part that was unclear. Rewrite your paragraph. After you make changes, read your paragraph to check the sentences with *and* and *but*. Did you use commas?

CHAPTER THREE

Retailing

Retailing is a major type of business all over the world. There are many kinds of retail stores for consumers to choose from: small shops and grocery stores to huge department stores and supermarkets.

Part 1
Vocabulary in Context

Content Vocabulary: Retailing

Add one word to complete each definition.

Example The ABC Store is a **chain**. There is an ABC Store in my town, and there are ABC stores in other cities all over the Northwest.

A **chain** has other stores in different __*places*__.

1. Some stores have a lot of **customer services**. When my mother broke her leg last Christmas, the department store helped her by choosing, wrapping, and mailing gifts for her. She paid a little more for these **services**. Another **customer service** is **delivery**. The department store **delivered** my dad's gift to the house by truck.

   Customer services help to make shopping _____.

   To **deliver** is to take to the correct _____.

2. There are many **convenience foods** at the supermarket. There is everything from spaghetti in a can to frozen pizza. All these foods are ready to heat and eat. They don't require a lot of time to cook.

   Convenience foods are foods that are easy to _____.

3. We are all **consumers**. When we buy something, we are **consuming**. I usually buy most of the **products** I use at the supermarket. Supermarkets have nonfood items such as soap and paper in addition to the food **products**. With many things at one store, the **consumer** saves time.

   A **consumer** is a person who buys __*products*__.

   Products are things that consumers __*buy*__.

4. There are many **retailers** in town. Some of them have huge department stores. Others have small shops with one special product such as shoes, cameras, or clothing. Most **retailers** work hard to make their stores clean and nice-looking.

A **retailer** is a person who owns a ___business___.

Subtechnical Vocabulary

Circle a, b, or c.

1. A discount house is a kind of store. Discount houses sell many different products **such as** clothes, stereos, electric appliances, paint, and shampoo at low prices.

   Such as introduces: a. general statements
                                    (b.) specific examples

2. There is a **variety** of products at a discount house. There are clothes, electronics, sports equipment, toys, and plants.

   Variety means: (a.) many different kinds
                        b. many products

3. My car got a flat tire on my way to the supermarket yesterday. I followed these **steps** to change it. First, I loosened the lug nuts, the small pieces of metal that hold the wheel on. Next, I jacked up the car, took off the lug nuts, and removed the bad tire. Then I put a new tire on and reversed these **steps.**

   Steps are: (a.) small parts of an action
                b. small pieces of metal

4. I picked up a magazine while I was in line at the supermarket. I read that in the Republic of Newcountry, **one out of ten** people (10% of the **population**) lives in the capital city.

   One out of twenty means: a. 50%
                                   b. 5%

   Population means: (a.) the number of people in a country
                                  b. a number of countries

5. I wanted to write a check for my groceries. The cashier asked, "Are you **familiar** with our check cashing rules? I need two pieces of identification, one with your signature."

   To be **familiar** with is: a. to pay with a check
                                (b.) to know about

6. I got a lottery ticket at the supermarket. The clerk added up the cost of all my food items and said, "$43.92, please." I asked, "Did you **include** the lottery ticket?"

   To **include** is to: a. talk about
                               b. buy
                               (c.) add together with other items

7. On my way back home, I stopped at the library for information about unemployment. The librarian said, "That information isn't **available** for this year. I can give you the numbers for last year."

   When something isn't **available**: a. it isn't important
                                       (b.) you can't get it
                                       c. you don't want it

8. This company is a book wholesaler, and it **distributes** books to bookstores and libraries in town. Businesses buy books; then someone from the company delivers the books to them.

   To **distribute** is to: a. send to someone you like
                               b. take to the correct people or places
                              (c.) take something away

Part 2
Reading

Warm-Up Activity: Skimming

Skimming (reading quickly for main ideas) gives readers a general idea of a piece of writing.

Skim the reading quickly and answer these questions. When you finish, discuss your answers in small groups and/or as a class.

1. What is the topic of the reading? _____retail stores_____

2. In which paragraph is the topic introduced? _____

3. Generally, a paragraph has one main idea. When writers finish one idea and start a new idea, they will also start a new paragraph. What is the main idea of paragraph 3? (*Circle one choice.*)
   a. Pecans are delicious nuts; they are good in pies and cookies.
   b. There are many kinds of retail stores, but usually only grocery stores and supermarkets sell frozen pecan pies.
   c. There are several changes from the time a food product is grown to the time it is ready to sell.

4. Reread paragraph 3. Put these steps in order. *(Write the numbers 1 through 5 in the blanks.)*

_____ The shells are removed.

_____ The pecans are distributed.

_____ Retailers receive and then sell the products.

_____ Farmers grow pecans.

_____ Nut products are made.

5. What are three major types of retail stores? Give an example of each.

_____

_____

_____

RETAIL STORES

1   Of the total working population in the United States, one out of eight people works in retailing. There is a great variety in the kinds and sizes of retail stores. Retailers sell everything from paper clips to tractors. Retail stores can be the small "mom and pop" grocery store on the corner or the giant chain with large stores throughout the nation.

2   There are many different types of retail stores. Department stores, chain stores, supermarkets, and discount houses are familiar examples. There are differences in products and services in these stores. At a department store, for example, the merchandise is more expensive and services such as delivery are available. At a discount house, the prices are low, and customer services are few. Specialty stores are another type of retail store. These stores usually sell only one kind of product, such as shoes, books, or clothing. Specialty stores include hobby shops, drugstores, barbershops, butcher shops, beauty shops, and travel agencies.

3   How does a product get to the retail outlet? There are several steps before a product is ready for the retailer. A convenience food, frozen pecan pie, can be an example. Farmers grow pecans; the pecans are then shipped to a company where the shells are removed. This company also distributes the nuts. It sends them to bakeries, nut companies, and candy companies where products such as pies, cakes, cookies, and nut candies are made. Bakeries sell these products to retailers: bakery shops, candy stores, grocery stores, and supermarkets. Pecan pies are delivered to retailers, ready for the customer to buy.

Part 3
Understanding Through Writing

General Comprehension: Identifying True and False Statements

Write T (true) or F (false).

_____ 1. Most retail stores sell pretty much the same products.

_____ 2. A chain has many different kinds of stores.

_____ 3. Specialty stores usually sell just one type of product.

_____ 4. Frozen dinners are an example of a convenience food.

Word Study

Write words from the reading.

1. What word at the beginning of paragraph 2 means **kinds**? _Different_

2. **Products** are things that result from work. Products come from the farm or the factory. See the middle of paragraph 2. What is the word for products for sale in a store? _Merchandise_

3. See the beginning of paragraph 3. What is the expression for **retail store**? _o·lo_

4. a. A **consumer** is a person who buys products. Write the word at the end of paragraph 3 with almost the same meaning. _customer_

     b. What difference do you see between a **consumer** and a **customer**?

     Consumer eat or use up - Customer = buyer

Sentence Study: Giving Information

Write complete sentence answers.

Example: How many people in the United States are in retailing?

One out of eight people is in retailing.

1. What are the five types of retail stores in the reading?

   Department stores, chain stores, supermarkets

   _____

2. Is a drugstore an example of a discount house or a specialty store?

   yes

3. What types of specialty stores do you use?

   Beauty shops, travel agency

4. In the second paragraph, there is a discussion of discount houses. What is an example of a discount house in your area?

   _____

5. In paragraph 3, frozen pecan pie is described. What kind of food is it?

   _____

Discourse Study: Noun Phrase Reference (*This, That, These, Those, The*)

Use *this, that, these,* and *those* instead of repeating a long phrase:

The factories in our city are places where clothing, food, and other kinds of products are made. **These factories** are usually located close to the river.

these factories = the factories in our city

There is a shoe factory across the river from our apartment. **That factory** produces tens of thousands of pairs of shoes every year.

that factory = the shoe factory across the river from our apartment.

The also signals a noun introduced before:

I like a store on 6th Street. **The store** has a lot of convenience foods.

the store = the store I just talked about, the one on 6th Street

The second time we read the word *store*, we know it is the store that we just talked about because of *the*. We understand that "a store on 6th Street" and "the store" are the same place.

See the reading to answer.

1. In paragraph 2, *these stores* is used two times. What does *these stores* mean the first time it is used?

   _____

2. What does it mean the second time?

   _____

3. Look at this sentence: Farmers grow pecans; **the pecans** are then shipped to a company where the shells are removed. What does **the pecans** mean? Complete this definition:

   the pecans = the pecans that _____

EXERCISE 1

Use **this, that, these,** or **those** to write more about these things and people. Work on a separate piece of paper.

Example: There are three **students** from my country at the university.

   These students are all in engineering.

1. There is a variety of **products** at this supermarket.
2. Convenience **foods** make life easy.
3. There is a world **leader** that I admire.
4. The capital **city** in my country is the center of government and business.
5. There is an unusual **store** down the street from me.
6. The world has three major **problems** today.
7. Transportation can be divided into several **types**.

Part 4
Getting Ready to Write Paragraphs

Describing: Noun + Noun, Adjective + Noun + Prepositional Phrase(s)

Noun + noun words tell the kind or type. They can be one word or two:

drugstore	music store
barbershop	tobacco shop
bookstore	coffee shop

Adjectives and prepositional phrases describe specifically:

Adjective	Noun	Prepositional Phrases
an expensive	store	around the corner from my sister
the little	grocery	at the corner of 9th Street and College Avenue
the gray	suit	in the window of the department store in town

Making Generalizations: *There* + *Be* and Present Tense

The topic sentence of paragraph is often a generalization with *there* + *be*

There are several stages in the life of a butterfly.
There is a nuclear power station near the metro area.

or with present tense:

Rooms with high ceilings **look** larger than they really are.
Water power **provides** energy to large parts of the Northwest.

Use *there* + *be* + a station (singular nouns)

some stations
a lot of stations (expressions of quantity)

three stations (numbers)

RECOGNITION EXERCISE

See the reading on page 34 to answer.

1. Write nine noun + noun words from the reading.

_____ _____ _____

_____ _____ _____

_____ _____ _____

2. Write the name of a store you go to and a noun + noun description of it.

   Example: _Sutherland's—a hardware store_
   Stater's — a Supermarket store

3. See paragraph 1 and find long noun phrases (five or more words). Write two complete phrases. (*Do not write complete sentences.*)

_____

_____

4. Write an original noun phrase with *a/an/the* + adjective + noun + prepositional phrase(s).

   Example: _the new barbershop at the corner of 10th and Main_

_____

5. In the sentence, "There is great variety in the kinds and sizes ....", the quantity is *great* (= "a lot"). Find sentences in paragraphs 2 and 3 with *there* + *be* + quantity. Write the two quantity expressions.

_____   _____

6. Write a generalization about retail stores. Use *there* + *be* + quantity.

_____

EXERCISE 2

*Read paragraphs 1–3. The topic sentences are missing. Write topic sentences for them (generalizations with **there** + **be** or present tense).*

1. _____
_____ First, managers must make sure that workers have enough work to do. A good manager gives enough work but not too much. A second point is that office work is difficult when workers are doing the same things over and over again. Managers must decide how to interest people in doing careful work and how to add variety to people's jobs.

2. _____
_____ You can write letters to your U.S. Senator or Congressperson telling how you feel about a particular problem. You can telephone or send a telegram when something important comes up for a vote. Public opinion is important to elected officials, and they listen to what people tell them. Another way to make your opinion known is to work for an organization. Major cities have all kinds of organizations. An organization can usually voice an opinion more effectively than an individual.

3. _____
_____ One thing to think about is the size. If your dictionary is a large and heavy, you may not have it with you when you need it. A pocket dictionary is helpful in this situation, but small dictionaries don't have many words. Something else to think about is whether to get a monolingual or bilingual dictionary. When you are ready for a monolingual dictionary, should you get a college or a learner's dictionary? A college dictionary has more information, but a learner's dictionary has easier definitions.

EXERCISE 3

Use one word or phrase in each list to make up eight long noun phrases. Do not use any word or phrase more than once. Write your long nouns as the subjects for eight completely different sentences.

Example: _The little boy in the room down the hall is trying to play the_

trumpet.

Adjectives	Nouns	Prepositional Phrases
tall	man	in the Student Union
√little	woman	in (country)
interesting	store	√in the room down the hall
unusual	student	in the shopping center
typical	clerk	√on 10th Street
grocery√	professor	at the large desk
clothing	teacher	in my major field
nice-looking	classmate	in my writing class
funny	person	with glasses
intelligent √	girl	with a briefcase
helpful	shop	with a beard
grouchy	√boy	at the party

Part 5
Writing Paragraphs

Warm-Up Activity: Paragraph Organization

These are some of the ways to organize paragraphs in English:

Description: A paragraph of description tells about something using adjectives and descriptive phrases. The topic is usually specific. *Examples:* the economic situation today in Montreal; my hotel room in Siena.

Description of a Process: A paragraph that describes a process tells the changes, actions or steps when something happens or develops. *Examples:* how to remember facts; unloading luggage from a passenger jet.

Narration: In a paragraph of narration, the writer tells a story from beginning to end (in chronological or time order). *Examples:* the first trip to the moon; the history of the car industry in Korea.

Classification: A paragraph of classification tells how a general class can be divided into groups. *Example:* Convenience foods can be frozen (TV dinners, pizza, desserts), fresh (sandwiches, cold cuts, salads), canned (spaghetti, soup), or bottled (baby food, sauces).

Explanation: A paragraph of explanation tells about or explains something. It gives reasons. *Examples:* why a telecopier is useful in business; the importance of critical thinking skills in the physical sciences.

What kinds of paragraphs are in the reading?

1. Paragraph 1 _____

2. Paragraph 2 _____

3. Paragraph 3 _____

Deciding on a Topic: Paragraphs of Description

Think about and decide on a topic from these suggestions:

1. Imagine that you are standing in the center of your capital city (*or another city you know well*). **Point out and describe** the places of interest.
2. **Describe** something you know well: a personal possession (*a telephone, car, piece of clothing*); a piece of equipment (*a computer, photocopier, etc.*); a place (*a vacation spot, a favorite place in this area, etc.*).
3. **Classify and describe** kinds of retail stores in your country or city. Give examples of each type. Are there any types that are common there but uncommon in (*the United States*)?

Brainstorming: Freewriting for Ideas

Freewriting helps writers to think of ideas. To freewrite is to write anything you can think of about your topic. The purpose is to let ideas come freely from writing. It is important **not** to think about grammar or spelling when you freewrite.

Write your topic at the top of a piece of paper. Then freewrite for 10 minutes. Use complete sentences, and try to fill the page with writing. Do not judge the importance of the ideas. Instead, let your mind think about the topic and write anything you think of. If you run out of ideas before the time is up, write anything at all: *I don't know what I want to say to describe this* or *I don't know what I want to say next.* Continue to write; you will think of more ideas.

Organizing Your Ideas

Read your freewriting paper two or three times. Underline interesting ideas. Write a list of the ideas; try to add one more idea to your list. Then decide on an order for the ideas and write a topic sentence for the paragraph. Use *there + be* or present tense. Tell what you will describe.

Explain to your partner what you are going to write about. Let your partner read your list of ideas and topic sentence. Your partner will ask you questions. This will help you to think of more ideas.

Writing a First Draft

Write a first draft of the paragraph. Begin with your topic sentence. Think only about getting the ideas down on paper. Continue writing until you are finished with the paragraph.

Editing

Editing is an important skill for writers. Good editing helps writers to state ideas clearly.

Use the following checklist to edit this paragraph about Newcountry. Rewrite the paragraph on a separate piece of paper. Then discuss your changes with a group of students.

From the top of Newcountry's Monument of 1965, there is a beautiful view of Newcity. To the north is the city center. That tall buildings to the east of the park are the city government offices. Just west of the park is the capitol building. The building is a brilliant white. It is many stories high. The building has many visitors every year. It was built in the early 1970s. It is the place of work for the president and government leaders. Looking south from the Monument, there is a large residential area. There are many houses and apartment buildings. The train station is to the far south. The airport lies to the west. All around the city is open countryside. It is an agricultural place. The capital city is surrounded by farms and small towns.

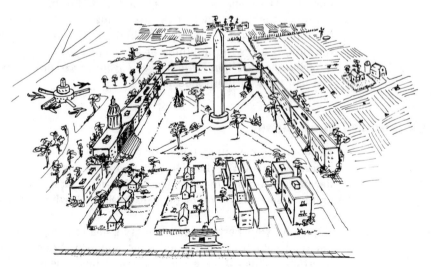

Now edit your first draft paper carefully. Go through each item of the checklist. Now is the time to correct grammar, spelling, and punctuation. Make the changes you want to, and copy the paragraph for your partner.

Read your partner's paper, and underline anything that isn't clear. Use the checklist to edit the paper. Discuss both papers using the checklist. Help your partner to rewrite any sentences that are unclear.

Checklist

1. What do you like best about the paragraph? Why?
2. Find a statement of what the writer is describing. Is it clear?
3. Find sentences of description. Add an adjective or a prepositional phrase where appropriate.
4. Look at the style of the paragraph. Which sentences can be combined with *and*, *but*, or a semicolon?
5. Where can the writer use *this/that*, *these/those*, and *the* instead of repeating phrases?
6. Read the paper one time for paragraph form and grammar. Then read it again for spelling and punctuation.

Revising the First Draft

Use your partner's suggestions to rewrite your paragraph. Try reading the paper aloud after you finish. Make any last changes you want to before handing it in.

CHAPTER FOUR

Library Research

Libraries provide up-to-date information on new inventions and discoveries. They also provide information about people and things that existed hundreds, thousands, or millions of years ago. Using libraries, we learn about people's highest achievements throughout time.

Part 1
Vocabulary in Context

Content Vocabulary: Library Research

Circle a or b.

1. Charlene's **research project** is about chemicals in food. She is getting books and articles at the library. If the research is interesting, she will probably write a paper.

   A **research project** means:
   a. a reference book or an article about chemicals in food
   b. work students do outside the classroom to learn about a topic

2. Her professor is working on a research project now. He is using **materials** such as journals, books, and interviews.

   Another example of **materials** is:
   a. an encyclopedia
   b. a research topic

3. The reference librarian is helping me with some government **documents** for my paper. I am using two reports and an article on population growth. I am getting many facts from these **documents**.

   Examples of **documents** are:
   a. letters, reports, articles
   b. facts, opinions, ideas, events

4. I decided to read the *New York Times* for the day of my birthday, 20 years ago. The librarian said that old newspapers were on **microfilm;** the newspapers themselves were too big for the library to keep.

Microfilm is:

    (a.) very small photographs of newspapers and other documents

    b. newspapers and other documents with very small photographs

5. Television news programs use **video-tape.** It is quick, easy, and cheaper than film. Both the picture and the sound are good quality, and a **video-tape** can be used over again.

    Videotape has:

    a. picture only

    (b.) picture and sound

6. The reference department has **indices** for articles in journals. With an **index**, you can find articles on any topic. The **index** gives an alphabetical list of topics. For each topic, there is a list of articles in different journals.

    An **index** is:

    (a.) a reference book that lists journal articles for many topics

    b. a reference book with many useful articles from journals

7. A **reference** is the information necessary to find a book or article at the library. For an article, the **reference** is the author and title of the article, the name of the journal, volume number, date, and pages.

    A **reference** is:

    (a.) information about an article or book

    b. information about how to use an index

8. One way to find information is to look in indices and write down all the interesting references. A second way is a **computer search**. You give the computer a topic and receive a list of references on the topic.

    A **computer search** means that:

    (a.) you look for the articles on your topic in indices

    b. a computer finds the articles on your topic

Subtechnical Vocabulary

Answer these questions.

1. A database is the information in a computer. When a computer's database is complete, its list of references will be complete also. When the database is incomplete, its list will be incomplete **as well.**

    What word in the second sentence means **as well**? *will be complete also*

2. Periods of time are sometimes named for **innovative** changes, for example, "the jet age" or "the computer age." The jet and the computer were put to use during these periods.

    Give an example of a recent **innovation** you have read or heard about.

    _____ *internet* _____

3. Success in school is **related to** long hours of study and hard work. One who studies hard will get good grades. Success in sports is **related to** good physical condition, coordination, and practice.

   What is success at work **related to**? *taking seriously his/her position*

4. Getting a good education is **worthwhile**. It takes a long time, but it is easy to see the value and importance of an education: You have a good job and many interests. The time and trouble of getting an education has **worthwhile** results.

   equal in value to
   being worth
   the time or effort
   spent.

   Give another example of a **worthwhile** activity. _____

5. "A lot of things **happened** while you were out of town. For one thing, the city finally cut down that tree across the street. Also, I completed my research paper. Oh, and your nephew won that long-distance race."

   Tell something of world importance that is **happening** now.

   _____

6. When Professor Porter lectures at the university, they **provide** her with a large room and any special equipment she needs. They don't always give her enough time, however.

   What word in the second sentence means **provide**? *give her a large room and any special equipment*

7. Latif wanted to go swimming, but Sam wanted to go on a picnic. They decided to **combine** both ideas and have a picnic at the beach.

   When you **combine** two ideas, do you separate them or join them together?

   _____ *join them together* _____

8. When you heat water to the boiling point, 100 degrees Celsius, you **produce** steam or water vapor. When you combine water, flour, and yeast, you **produce** dough for bread.

   The freezing point for water is 0 degrees Celsius. What do you **produce** when you freeze water?

   _____

9. The woman's idea was important, but the way she spoke to the famous professor was not **appropriate.** She was very informal, calling him by his first name and beginning with, "Hey, what's happening?"

What is **appropriate** at the White House: a suit or shorts? _Suit_

Part ❷
Reading

Warm-Up Activity: Discussion Questions

Discuss these questions together as a class.

1. What is your usual reason for using the library?
2. Have you ever done a research paper? What was the topic?
3. Will you do research papers in the future? What topic might be interesting for a research paper?
4. What do you do in the library when beginning a research paper?

TECHNOLOGICAL INNOVATIONS AT LIBRARIES

1   Like business and industry, the academic world is changing as technology advances. Libraries are one place we see these changes. Many innovative things are happening in both public and university libraries. Libraries are using new equipment and techniques for research, and librarians are teaching students the new techniques.

2   One service that some university libraries are now providing is a computer search of materials for students doing research. Before starting a research project, students check with their library to see if a computer search is worthwhile. This kind of search cannot help with all research projects, but it can save time if the topic is in the computer's database. When you are doing a manual search for a research paper, you look at all the indices appropriate to the research topic. You look up the words related to the topic in the indices. It takes many hours to look up this information and write down the references. A computer search is faster and easier. You and a reference librarian decide on the words to enter into the computer. For example, if the topic is *techniques of teaching reading to children*, you could use "teaching methods" and "reading—elementary school." Then the computer looks for these words in its database and gives you a list of references for your topic. A computer can take two or more ideas and produce references that combine those ideas. A computer search can also be more complete than a manual search.

3   College and university libraries are providing other technological services as well. For example, if students miss a lecture, often they can go to the library and watch a similar lecture on videotape. An-

Microfilm Reader-Printer. Photo courtesy of 3M.

other change is the frequent use of microfilm. Librarians are able to collect more material in one building by having newspapers, magazines, and other documents on microfilm. Students use microfilm readers in the library for these materials.

4   These innovations in libraries are helpful to library users, but they are also expensive. Many libraries are facing budget problems. There is more technology available today; as a result, libraries are paying higher costs for the equipment that makes research easier.

Part 3
Understanding Through Writing

General Comprehension

A. Mark these sentences T (true) or F (false).

_F_ 1. Research techniques are almost the same as they were 50 years ago.

_F_ 2. A computer search for materials is the best way to begin any type of research.

_T_ 3. A major disadvantage of a manual search is the length of time it takes.

_____T____ 4. When you don't do a computer search, you use indices to find articles on your topic.

_____T____ 5. Libraries have microfilm because it's easier to use than newspapers.

B. Reread these paragraphs. Circle one choice.

1. What is the main idea of paragraph 2?

   a. A manual search for materials takes a long time.

   b. A librarian can help choose words for the computer to look for.

   c. A computer search for materials has advantages over a manual search.

2. What is the main idea of paragraph 3?

   a. Newspapers and other documents are often on microfilm.

   b. Videotape and microfilm are two more technological services that libraries often have.

   c. Libraries are buying a lot of technological equipment these days.

3. What is the main idea of paragraph 4?

   a. Technological innovations in libraries are helpful but expensive.

   b. Libraries have budget problems because of the many library users.

   c. Technological equipment makes research easier for the library user.

Word Study

Write words from the reading.

1. What adjective in the middle of paragraph 1 means "new and different"?

   many

2. What word in paragraph 1 means "methods," "ways of doing something"?

   Innovative

3. What word in the middle of paragraph 2 describes a search done by hand, not by computer?

   manual

4. Read paragraph 4 again. When we say that libraries are having "budget problems," what kind of problems are these?

   income and expenses

5. What words in paragraph 4 suggest the meaning of "budget problems"?

   higher costs

Sentence Study: Identifying Synonymous Sentences

Circle the best restatement of the first sentence: a, b, or c. Discuss your answers in small groups and/or as a class.

Example: Like business and industry, the academic world is changing as technology advances.
    a. Technology in business and industry is progressing faster than in academics.
    b. In business and industry, technology is changing and advancing.
    ⓒ In academics, as well as in business and industry, technological advance is causing changes.

The first sentence points to technological change in three areas. Choice *a* says that the technological progress in two areas is faster than in the third. Choice *b* talks about change in two areas only; it does not say anything about academics. (Choice *b* is a correct statement, but it is not an accurate restatement.) Choice *c* restates the ideas of the first sentence: All three areas are changing because of advances in technology.

1. Before starting a research project, students check with their library to see if a computer search is worthwhile.

    a. It is useful to check at the library after doing a research project to find out about a computer search.
    b. Before research begins, students find out at the library if a computer search will be useful.
    c. Students need to go to the library for computer searches.

2. The computer searches its database for the words you enter into it and writes out a list of references for your topic.

    a. The computer looks through its information and finds references for your topic by looking at the words you entered.
    b. The computer looks through its database to choose your topic.
    c. The computer writes out a list of the words you entered.

3. Librarians are able to collect more material in one building by having newspapers and other documents on microfilm.

    a. Libraries have more newspapers and other documents on microfilm than is available in other university buildings.
    b. Librarians like to have newspapers and other documents on microfilm.
    c. Libraries can keep larger amounts of materials by having microfilm copies of newspapers and other documents.

4. A computer search cannot help with all research projects, but it can save time if the topic is in the computer's database.

    a. Computer searches are helpful with any research project.
    b. Computer searches are useless for most kinds of research.
    c. Computer searches can save time when the computer's database includes the research topic.

Discourse Study: Noun Phrase Reference

See the reading to write the meanings of these phrases. (The numbers in parentheses tell which paragraph to look at for each phrase.)

Example: (1) these changes = _technological changes in the academic world_

1. (2) this kind of search = _____

2. (2) these words = _____

3. (2) those ideas = _____

4. (3) these materials = _____

5. (4) these innovations = _____

Part 4
Getting Ready to Write Paragraphs

The Present Progressive (Be + V-ing)

The present progressive means **at this moment**:

He **is taking** a shower. Can I have him call you back?

these days/currently:

I**'m reading** a great book.

and **in the near future**:

We**'re going** downtown this afternoon.

The time meaning **these days/currently** is the most common in writing:

Informal: I**'m having** a great time at work **these days.** My boss **is giving** me a lot of interesting things to do.

Formal: Gifts to the library **are increasing. Currently,** the library **is receiving** a lot more money than in past years.

Irregular Plurals

Words from Latin and Greek have irregular plurals:

Singular	Plural	Singular	Plural
appendix	appendices	thesis	theses
index	indices (indexes)	analysis	analyses
datum	data	parenthesis	parentheses

RECOGNITION EXERCISE

See the reading on page 47 to answer.

1. Look at the progressive verbs in paragraph 1 of the reading. What time do they all refer to: *at this moment*, *currently*, or *in the near future*?

   _____currently_____

2. Write the word in paragraph 2 with the plural of *datum*. Write the other foreign plural in this paragraph also.

   _data,_____indices_____ _____

3. Write an original sentence with a Latin or Greek plural.

   Example: __Indices usually have many volumes._____

   _____

4. Write irregular plurals. Then underline words that tell the meaning.

   Example: Peter and Charlene are working on master's degrees. They are each

   writing a <u>long paper</u> called a **thesis**. They need to finish their

   _____theses_____ before receiving their degrees.

   a. Sometimes Peter uses a **parenthesis** when he writes. (There is a **parenthe-**
   sis on both ends of a note like this. The note usually explains something in the
   writing.) Peter knows that it is not a good idea to use ___parentheses___ a
   lot in formal writing, however.

   b. Charlene wants to do a careful **analysis** in her paper. Both students will look
   at their topics in detail to understand them. If their ___analyses___ are
   well done, maybe their theses will be published.

   c. Charlene is including an **appendix** at the end of her paper. In the **appendix,**
   she will give some statistical information about her topic. Peter doesn't have
   any ___appendices___ in his paper.

EXERCISE 1

On a separate piece of paper, write one or more sentences for each item.
*Use **be** + **V-ing.***

   Example: Describe your activity at the moment.

   __Right now I am watching the news on TV.__

1. Describe your activity at the moment.
2. Describe one of your most important current activities.

3. Describe the current activity of a family member.
4. What is a current activity of the government of your country?
5. Describe a current activity of another country in your area of the world.
6. Describe a current problem of world importance. What are countries of the world doing to improve the situation?

Part 5
Using Two-Word Verbs

Study these two-word verbs with *look*:

1. *Look up* = (1) "raise one's head," or (2) "use a reference book"

   He **looked up** when she walked into the room.
   He **looked up** the word *synopsis* in the dictionary.

2. *Look at* = (1) "use one's eyes," or (2) "study"

   She **looked at** me for a moment.
   She **looked at** his term paper for two and one-half hours.

3. *Look over* = "examine quickly"

   She **looked over** my thesis but didn't read it completely.

4. *Look after* = "take care of"

   I can **look after** your daughter today when you go to the dentist.

5. *Look for* = "search for," "try to find"

   They **looked for** her car keys for ten minutes.

6. *Look in on* = "visit someone who is sick"

   My uncle is not well. I will **look in on** him tomorrow afternoon.

EXERCISE 2

*Write a two-word verb with **look** in each blank.*

1. Barbara and Cathy are going to the nursery to buy some plants and seeds for a vegetable garden. Cathy wants to be sure to get the next bus, so she

   looks at the bus schedule carefully.

2. As the women walk to the bus stop, they talk about the kinds of vegetables they want to grow. Suddenly the bus arrives and they _look up_ because of the loud noise.

3. After they arrive at the nursery, Barbara suggests, "Let's ___look over___ the different kinds of flowers for a minute too, OK?"

4. Cathy wants to find a special kind of squash. She says, "It's not summer squash and it's not yellow squash. I forget the name. Will you help me ___look for___ it?"

5. When they get back to their apartment, Barbara says, "Would you ___look after___ the tomato plants and give them some water? I would like to ___look in on___ my neighbor. She has been sick."

Part 6
Writing Paragraphs

Warm-Up Activity: Limiting the Topic

A paragraph has a general topic sentence and supporting information. Paragraphs in English are short, usually six to twelve sentences. If the topic is too large, it is hard to be specific. By choosing a smaller topic or discussing only one part of a larger one, writers can give specific information.

*Are topics 1 to 6 better for paragraphs or books? Write **paragraph** or **book** in each blank.*

1. ___book___ vacation spots around the world
2. ___paragraph___ a deep sea fishing trip in Australia
3. ___book___ how to use an index in the library
4. ___book___ the life and times of Henry Ford
5. ___paragraph___ techniques in retailing
6. ___paragraph___ the ideal supermarket

Write two paragraph topics for each large subject area.

Example techniques in retailing

    advertising for specialty shops

    types of nonfood items in supermarkets

1. the agricultural products of my country

    _____

    _____

2. how to use a computer

    _____

    _____

3. an international student's impressions of the United States

    _____

    _____

Discuss your answers in pairs. Are any of the topics still too large for a paragraph? Think of two smaller paragraph topics for one or two ideas.

Example: advertising for specialty shops

    effective newspaper advertising

    how to use special offers to increase sales

Choosing a Topic

In this section, you will write a paragraph of explanation or description. You will talk to someone else to get information for your paragraph. Choose a topic from among these suggestions.

1. **Describe** a piece of equipment at your library. Go to the library to get information about it: what it looks like, where it is located in the library, what it is used for, how much it is used. Ask a librarian to show you how to use it. Think of one or two more questions to ask. Use the equipment yourself.
2. **Classify** and **describe** the types of materials at your campus library. At the library, ask for an information sheet that describes the library and its holdings. Ask a reference librarian what types of materials there are. Does the library have newspapers, microfilm, microfiche, videotapes, records, and photographs? Are there group study rooms, typewriters, and computers for students? Ask one or two more questions.
3. Watch the activity at your campus library. **Describe** the things that are happening. Use the present progressive. Then **describe** how

the activity is similar to or different from what happens at libraries in your country. For more information, ask students in class how the library is similar to or different from the ones they use at home.

4. **Explain** some things a new student at your school needs to know about. What have you learned about campus life that is important to you? What are the best facilities on campus (*the recreation center, the library, the restaurant at the Student Union*)? Interview two or three students in your class to find out their answers to these questions.

5. **Explain** a current theory in your major field. Are opinions divided on any questions at present? Speak to a professor or a student in your field; ask questions about your topic. Find out his or her opinion.

Brainstorming for Ideas: Writing Words and Phrases

Write your topic at the top of a piece of paper. Write down any words and phrases you can think of for your topic. Think only about your topic. Don't worry about spelling or complete sentences; just write down words as quickly as possible. Work individually for about five minutes. When you are finished brainstorming, your paper might look like this:

Exchange papers with a partner. Add two or three words to your partner's paper. Then check your paper to see if you agree with the additions.

Begin to think about a main idea for the paragraph. Make a list of questions to ask other students, a librarian, or a professor at your school. Share your questions with your partner. Give your partner any advice you can.

Talk to a librarian, a professor, or other students. Ask your questions. Take notes during the conversation, or write down some notes right after you finish talking. The discussion will give you more ideas to work with. After the discussion, decide firmly on the main idea of your paragraph.

Getting Organized

Review the parts in a paragraph:

First sentence or two:	Introduce the topic and main idea; tell why the topic is important.
Discussion:	Describe, explain, or classify.
	Help your readers to understand the main idea.
Last sentence or two:	Finish your discussion of the main idea.

Look at your brainstorming paper with words and phrases. Put them in groups. Which group is the largest? Write a topic sentence about the words in the largest group.

Study the notes that you took during your conversation with other students, a librarian, or a professor. Reread your topic sentence. Does it state the main idea that you want to discuss? If not, change it. Make a short list of the things that you want to talk about in the paragraph.

In pairs, tell what you plan to say in your paragraph. Show your partner your topic sentence and list. Ask if your paragraph topic is small enough. Your partner's questions will help you to make ideas clear.

Writing a First Draft

Use your list to write a first draft of your paragraph. Get down the ideas now; you can check later for spelling, punctuation, etc. Think about the purpose of each section: introducing, discussing, and concluding. In the discussion, focus on your more specific purpose: describing or explaining. Use *this/that, these/those* for reference.

Joining Sentences

Use the suggestions in a-f to join phrases and sentences in items 1–11. Write your sentences as a paragraph on a separate piece of paper. Then compare paragraphs in pairs.

√ a. Combine Sentences 1 and 2. (Join phrases with *and*.)
   b. Write Sentence 3 without changes.
   c. Combine Sentences 4 and 5 with a semicolon and *also*.
   d. Write Sentence 6 without changes.
   e. Combine Sentences 7 and 8 with *but*. Add a phrase from Sentence 9 using *and*.
   f. Combine Sentences 10 and 11 with *but*.

Example: *Hometown University Library spends thousands of dollars every year on improvements and new equipment.*

1. Hometown University Library spends thousands of dollars every year on improvements.
2. Hometown University Library spends thousands of dollars every year on new equipment.
3. A recent improvement is a computerized card catalog system.
4. This system finds books at Hometown and other local libraries.
5. It shows which books are checked out.
6. Having the right materials available is important in research.
7. Hometown University's computerized system offers people immediate information about books in all local libraries.
8. Librarians find that students continue to use the regular card catalog.
9. Librarians find that students go to other local libraries when a book is not on the shelf.
10. Technology is changing research techniques in the United States.
11. It takes time for people to learn about the new techniques.

Editing

Now edit your paper using the following checklist. Remember to join some of the sentences in the paragraph. Make changes and copy the paragraph for another student to read.

Exchange papers with your partner, and use the checklist to edit the paper. Underline any part you have a question about. Discuss your papers together using the checklist. Help your partner to rewrite any part that is unclear.

Checklist

1. What part of the paragraph do you like best? Why?
2. Find the main idea of the paragraph. Is the writer's purpose clear?
3. Do you suggest taking out any part to limit the paragraph?
4. What else could you add to help explain, describe, or classify?
5. Where can you join sentences with *and, but, because,* or a semicolon?
6. Find clear examples of *this/that, these/those.*

7. Check the verbs in every sentence. Do you understand the time meaning of each verb?
8. Read the paper again for spelling and punctuation.

Revising the First Draft

Rewrite your paragraph to hand in. Remember your partner's questions and suggestions. You may want your partner, another student, or a group of students to read or listen to your paper again before you hand it in.

Making an Orientation Guide for New Students

After you receive comments from your teacher and rewrite your paragraph, work as a class to decide on the most useful paragraphs to put in a guide for new students at your school.

CHAPTER FIVE

City Life

Living in a city and living in the countryside suggest two very different ways of life. In the country, the concern may be how to keep animals fed and crops growing in the field. Nature has an effect on people's yearly income. Workers in cities have greater choices: They can get training and work in different kinds of jobs, live in many types of housing, and enjoy a variety of entertainment.

Part 1
Vocabulary in Context

Content Vocabulary: City Life

Circle a or b.

1. Most cities have small areas called **districts**. **Districts** usually have different kinds of people, but sometimes they consist of people who belong to a similar religious, racial, cultural, or economic group.

   A **district** is: a. a part of a city

   b. a group of similar people

2. Our **neighborhood** is growing larger. There is a new grocery store two blocks south, and several houses are going up on our street. The tennis courts in the park are almost complete now too.

   A **neighborhood** is: a. two or three new houses

   b. a small part of a city district

3. There are several **freeways** in the downtown area. They allow people to go quickly by car from one part of the city to another part. People use the north/south **freeway** when going through town.

   A **freeway** is: a. a large road for fast travel by car

   b. a road that goes north and south

4. People are moving out of the city center and into the **suburbs**. In the city, you have more entertainment and restaurants. In the **suburbs**, you have cleaner, quieter streets and fewer people, but less entertainment.

   A **suburb** is: a. a place with no entertainment

   b. an area outside the city center where people live

5. People in the United States move often. Sometimes they don't want to, but their jobs require them to. It is always difficult to move. After time, **displaced** people feel more comfortable in the new place.

   Displaced people: a. have moved
                          b. stay in one area

Subtechnical Vocabulary

Give examples and answer questions.

1. A **concern** interests you and worries you. The main **concern** for a business is usually making money. Some people are **concerned** about the future of life on earth.

   Give an example of one of your **concerns**. *my concerned is my kid's education*

2. A **trend** shows change in a direction. In the 1950s and 60s, there was a **trend** toward a lot of money for space research in the United States. In the 70s and 80s, the **trend** was toward less money for space research.

   What is a new **trend** in music? *rap*

3. When you say there were **approximately** 12 people at the meeting, you are showing that the number is not exact, but it is close to the correct figure. The correct figure might be 11, 12, 13, or 14.

   Approximately how many people live in your hometown? _____

4. She will go to the local junior college **of necessity**. She doesn't have the money to go to a private university, and the state college is too far to drive every day. She has no other choice.

   When you do something **of necessity**, do you have several choices or only one choice?

   one choice

5. **Unlike** many countries of the world, Australia is surrounded by water.

   From this example, does **unlike** show difference or similarity? *difference*

6. **According to** shows the authority for factual information. The authority may be a book, a person, or any other source of information.

   Write the authority for the information in the following sentence: **According to** the boss, it's going to be a busy week.

7. **As for** means the same as **with regard to** and **in reference to**. All three point out a topic that will be discussed more specifically.

Fill in a noun phrase: We are working as quickly as possible on the report. **As for** _Vision book_, I'm not sure I can tell you at the moment. We need another week before I can tell you exactly when we'll finish.

Part 2
Reading

Warm-Up Activity: Discussion Questions

Discuss these questions in small groups or as a class. Ask each other more questions during the discussion.

1. Are progress and change positive things?
2. What is a recent example of progress or change that has had positive results for people generally?
3. Can you think of a recent example of progress that caused problems?
4. Describe life in the city where you are now living.

Now read the informal letter on page 63.

Part 3
Understanding Through Writing

General Comprehension

Work on these questions individually; then discuss them in small groups.

1. Why did Jesse write this letter to his friend Jack? What is the problem he wanted to tell Jack about?

   _____

2. Write the most general sentence (the topic sentence) in paragraph 3. (A topic sentence comes at the beginning, middle, or end of a paragraph.)

   _____

3. Is Jesse a younger or an older man? Write the words that tell you.

   _____

AN INFORMAL LETTER

> Monday, June 21
>
> Dear Jack,
>
> 1 Lots of things happening in the city these days. The biggest concern for most people around here is this trend with the city government to destroy old neighborhoods. Jack, they're going to tear down our neighborhood! They're going to tear down these walls and build a darn freeway! Can you believe it? Approximately seventy-five families are going to be displaced. Both Marge and I are very upset.
>
> 2 They're going to start on Landers Street and work North. All of our little district here is going to be destroyed. The corner grocery store where Marge meets the other women around here. The little park where I sit and talk with my friends — everything. Marge and I have to move out by the end of the month.
>
> 3 We feel lucky in a way because we have enough money to move — some people in this old neighborhood live here of necessity. These people have nowhere to go and no money to get there. And a lot of the people in this neighborhood are old like us. How are they going to feel comfortable in a new place? Unlike many of these folks, we have family close by to help us. But we keep thinking that all our friends for the last twenty-three years are going to be spread out all over the city. No more bridge on the weekends at Mac and Sally's. They're going to move out to the suburbs. No more drinking with the guys at Gary's Place. Gary's Place isn't going to be there. As for the guys, who knows where they're all going to be? It's going to be hard for everyone.
>
> 4 Hope things are better for you. Are you feeling well these days? According to the newspaper, they're going to begin on Landers Street in about three weeks. Why don't you come for a visit before then? Marge and I would like to see you. You could visit us either here real soon or at our new place in a month or so. I'll call this weekend.
>
> Jesse

4. What do you think Jesse and Marge will miss most when they move?

_____ Underline parts of the reading that show this idea.

5. Why is it necessary for Jesse and Marge to leave their home? Can you think of any other way that a city could handle this problem?

_____

6. This letter from Jesse is informal style. Are letters between friends informal in your language too?

_____

Word Study

Write words from the reading.

1. Write the pronoun in the first paragraph meaning "decision makers," "people in control."

_____

2. Write the word in the third paragraph meaning "relaxed."

_____

3. Write the two-word verb in the middle of the third paragraph meaning "distribute over a large area."

_____

4. Write the expression toward the end of the third paragraph that means "at the home of two people." (The two names are given.)

_____

5. What two expressions in the fourth paragraph give approximate times? (Look for words with the meaning "approximately."

_____

Sentence Study: Sentence Fragments

A fragment is an incomplete sentence with no subject or an incomplete verb. In formal writing, fragments are not used. In informal writing (or conversation), it is fine to use them:

"Not much going on."   = There isn't much going on. (OR)
                                     Not much (activity) is going on.
"Do you know Marge?"
"Yes, a lovely person."   = She is a lovely person.

Write these fragments as complete sentences. See the reading for the context. Then discuss your sentences with a partner.

Example: Lots of things happening in the city these days.

Lots of things are happening in the city these days.

1. The corner grocery store where Marge meets the other women around here.

_____

_____

2. The little park where I sit and talk with my friends.

_____

3. No more bridge on the weekends at Mac and Sally's.

_____

4. Hope things are better for you.

_____

Part **4**
Getting Ready to Write Letters

Informal Writing Style

These items are usual in informal writing but not in formal writing:

1. Conjunctions (*and, but, or*) at the beginning of sentences:

   But we keep thinking that all our friends are going to be spread out all over the city.

2. Sentence fragments instead of complete sentences:

   Lots of things **happening** in the city these days.

3. Informal words and expressions:

   real soon/**nowhere to go and no money to get there**

4. A personalized style:

   Jack, they're going to tear down **our** neighborhood.

5. Exclamation points, dash instead of semicolon (or commas), short forms (contractions) instead of full forms:

   They**'re** going to tear down these walls**!**
   We feel lucky in a way because we have enough money to move—some people in this old neighborhood live here of necessity.

Or, Either . . . Or

Or works like *and*, joining phrases and clauses. *Or* shows two possibilities:

Is Mac **or** Sally going to speak for our group at the meeting?
Mac could talk forcefully, **or** Sally could speak diplomatically.

Either . . . or also introduces two possibilities:

Either Mac **or** Sally is going to speak at the meeting.

Maybe Mac will speak at the meeting; maybe Sally will. No one has decided. What is decided is this: Only one person will go, and Mac and Sally are good choices. One of them will go.

Use *either . . . or* when you are not sure of the facts:

The meeting is **either** on Tuesday **or** on Thursday. I can't remember which day, but it's certainly not Wednesday or Friday.

The words after *either* and *or* must be the same form: nouns with nouns, verbs with verbs, etc. What parts of speech are joined in these examples?

Either **Mac** or **Sally** is going to go to the meeting.
The meeting will be either **at the lawyer's office** or **at City Hall**.
We are going to either **win completely** or **get most of what we want**.

When one subject is singular and one is plural, the subject next to the verb determines its form:

Either my neighbors or **Sam is** going to attend the meeting.
Either Sam or **my neighbors are** going to attend the meeting.

RECOGNITION EXERCISE

See the reading on page 63 to answer. Discuss your work with a partner.

1. Find the sentence with *either ... or* in the fourth paragraph. What are the words joined by *either ... or* in this example?

   _____

2. Write an original sentence in which you combine two times with *either . . . or.*

   _____

3. Write the informal sentence in the third paragraph with the conjunction *and* at the beginning.

   _____

4. Here are some informal expressions from the reading. Write the same idea in a more formal style.

   Examples: most people around here ___*most people in this area*___

   our little district here ___*this district*_____

   a. these walls _____

   b. these folks _____

c. the guys _____

d. a month or so _____

EXERCISE 1

*On a separate piece of paper, use **either ... or** to join sentences.*

> *SITUATION:* Jesse and Marge's daughter has four children in school. The oldest is Brenda. Brenda has one sister and two brothers.

> *Example:* Maybe Brenda is a student at City College.
> Maybe her sister is a student at City College.

>   *Either Brenda or her sister is a student at City College.*

1. Maybe Brenda leaves for school at 7:30. Maybe she leaves at 7:00.
2. Maybe Brenda is majoring in physics, or perhaps she is majoring in political science.
3. Maybe her brothers are going to take some night classes. Maybe her sister is going to take some night classes.
4. Maybe Brenda is getting straight As. Maybe she's getting As and Bs.
5. Maybe Brenda is going to graduate this year. Perhaps her brothers are going to graduate this year.

EXERCISE 2

*On a separate piece of paper, answer by joining sentences with **either ... or**.*

> *Example:* Will the city council change next year?

> Maybe it will change a little next year.
> It could also stay about the same next year.

>   *It will either change a little or stay about the same.*

1. Why don't we see much progress from the council?

   The members might be lazy.
   They might be uninterested in city business.

2. Who do you think can help?

   It's possible that the mayor can help in this situation.
   Another person who can probably help is the police chief.

3. Why don't the people in this city elect a better city council?

   Maybe the people are unaware.
   Possibly they just don't care.

4. What do the members do at meetings?

   They hear committee reports.
   They form more committees.

5. Do you have any ideas?

The people need to demand good work from council members.
The people need to throw the bums out.

Part 5
Writing Letters

Warm-Up Activities

Using One Topic per Paragraph

All the sentences in a paragraph discuss one main idea. In formal writing
other ideas are not discussed in the same paragraph. A strong topic sentence helps the writer to stay with the topic. Does this paragraph discuss
one or more than one main idea?

> I have some interesting plans for next summer. First of all, I'm
> going to work for a month and one-half as a part-time reporter. Jour-
> nalism is exciting to me; I know this work is going to be fun and
> instructive. I'm also going to visit my Aunt Harriet on Cape Cod in
> Massachussetts. Poor Aunt Harriet is very ill. Her doctor says that
> she needs more exercise. I think she needs someone to talk to. I'm
> going to try to be helpful to her. Everyone in the family is worried
> about her health.

These are the main points in the beginning of the paragraph:

topic: plans for next summer

— work as a reporter
— visit to Aunt Harriet

After Aunt Harriet is introduced, the writer changes to a discussion of Aunt
Harriet's health. This is not a "plan for next summer." Instead, it is a
different topic altogether. If the paragraph is going to be about Aunt Harriet's health, it should begin with a different topic sentence that introduces
this subject.

Writing Business Letters

Business letters have formal writing style. There are six parts in a business letter: date, address, salutation (Dear Dr. Smith), body, closing (Sincerely, Sincerely yours, Yours truly, Respectfully yours), and signature.
Find these parts in the following letter. Note the colon (:) after the salutation. In letters to friends, a comma is used instead.

SITUATION: You're applying to a school in an English-speaking country. Complete this letter to the admissions office.

Write a beginning paragraph which tells if you're a graduate
or undergraduate, where you're from, where you're studying

now, what your major is, what degree program you're interested in, and any other important personal information. Fill in the other information, and sign your name at the end.

_____   _____
                                          (date)

_____
_____
          (university address)

Dear Sir or Madam:

_____

_____

_____

_____

_____

I would like to receive a catalog and an application for

_____ study. If there is a special bulletin for the

Department of _____, please send this also. En-

closed please find $6.00 to cover the cost of the catalog and

postage.

My address is:

_____ (name)

_____ (street address)

_____ (city, state, zip code)

Thank you very much.

                                  Sincerely,

                                  _____
                                          (signature)

Choosing a Topic: Formal and Informal Letters

Business letters are formal; they are direct and brief. A letter to a friend is informal; it includes personal information. Read these suggestions and decide on a letter that you need to write.

Request some information from a school: when they need your
transcripts and TOEFL scores, for example.

Request a favor. (Do you need letters of recommendation for the
schools to which you are applying? Do you want the director of
your language school to telephone an admissions office in support
of your application?)

Write to an English-speaking friend. Tell about life in the city
where you are now living.

Complain about a product or service.

Write to a politician or famous person.

Brainstorming for Ideas: Listing Main Points

Write a list of the main points you plan to discuss in the letter. Then read
your list. Which points will you discuss together? Put the points into
groups. These points are for a four-paragraph letter of complaint.

Example:

personal information:

What problem is

> foreign student from Indonesia
> live within walking distance of your restaurant
> eat at your restaurant all the time, but recent problem

why we chose your restaurant:

> wanted to take our friends to a nice place
> food is great
> service is quick
> good children's menu

what happened:

> my family arrived with two Swedish guests at 6:30
> placed our order at 6:45; our next door neighbors sat down at 7:00
> at 7:45, neighbors were finished; we had not received our meal

results:

> everyone hungry and grouchy, kids were noisy
> we will not be back

After you organize your points in groups like this, show your notes to partner and find out if the ideas are clear and well organized.

Writing a First Draft

When you are writing your first draft, think only about getting the ideas on paper. Follow the organization in your notes, and continue writing until you finish the letter. If possible, use *either . . . or* in the letter.

Revising the Letter

Check all the sentences of each paragraph; make sure they discuss the main ideas of those paragraphs. If you are writing a business letter, make sure you come to your main point briefly and directly. Use the following checklist to edit your paper. Then make changes and copy it over.

Exchange papers with your partner; use the checklist to edit the letter you receive. Underline anything that you have a question about. Discuss both letters together. Help your partner to rewrite anything that isn't clear. Then use your partner's suggestions to revise your letter to hand in.

Checklist

1. To whom is the letter going to be sent? Is it formal or informal?
2. What is the writer's purpose in writing this letter? Is the purpose clear from the beginning?
3. If it is a business letter, find examples of formal writing. If it is a letter to a friend, find examples of informal writing.
4. Do all the sentences of each paragraph discuss one main idea? Do you suggest adding or taking out anything?
5. Read the paragraph one time for form. Check that each part of the letter is clear (the date, salutation, etc.). Then read the letter a second time to check spelling, punctuation, and use of *either . . . or.*

CHAPTER SIX

Solar Energy

The industrialized countries have energy problems. The problems involve both environmental pollution and energy dependency. Scientists are looking beyond usual sources of energy because of these problems. For one major energy use — home heating — solar energy may provide a source of nonpolluting energy in many areas. The use of solar energy to produce electricity is also a possibility for the future.

Part 1
Vocabulary in Context

Subtechnical Vocabulary

Answer the questions. Where there is a choice, circle one answer.

1. Apples **come from** apple trees. Success **comes from** hard work. What **comes from** the sun?

   Solar energy, light

2. "We buy equipment from Central Equipment, Inc. What's your **source**?"
   "All our equipment comes from Crosstown Equipment Supply."

   Add a verb: A **source** is the place that something _____
   come from

3. We need that equipment, but the saleswoman cannot sell it to us right now because it is **in short supply**. She will receive more next week, and we can get it then.

   If something is **in short supply**, is there a large amount available?

   no   is no having enough, not long.
   available

4. "What exactly is a word processing **system**? Isn't it just one machine?"
   "No, there's a computer, a disk drive, keyboard, TV screen, and printer. These different pieces of equipment work together as a **system**." _yes. arrangement of units that fuction together._

   Write the one sentence above that explains **system**.

   adapt. way thing   method, way.

5. We have an interesting research idea but are going to need **funding** from the government because the research will be expensive.

   What is another word for **funding**? _____ *money* _____

6. A **majority** means "more than half."

   Which percentage is a **majority**? a. 33% b. 47% c. 54%

7. "This man wants to know how much our heating bill is. He's interested in our **rate of consumption** because of our solar home." "Well, the bill this month is about $72. Is he interested in past rates too, or only the **current rate** of use?"

   a. What word above means the opposite of **current**? *past*   ~~present~~

   b. If someone wants to know the **rate** of energy use, he wants to know: *amount*

      1. how much is used per month
      2. what time of day they usually turn on the heater

   c. What word means the same as **consumption**? *consume*

Word Opposites

Discuss these word opposites (antonyms) as a class. Then use **one pair** *of antonyms to fill in all the blanks in each numbered item. Where there is a choice, circle one answer.*

✓ active – passive	top – bottom
basic – complicated	finite – infinite
direct – indirect	heating – cooling
rise – fall	polluting – nonpolluting

Example: Someone who tries to change people's opinions is ___*active*___ in

decision-making. A person who lets others decide is more

___*passive*___.

A passive solar heating system:

a. uses moving parts powered by electricity
b. doesn't require electric equipment

1. You are at the corner of

   10th and Cedar and want

   to go to 12th and Spruce.

   You decide to walk down

   10th Street past Pine and

then down Spruce to 12th Street. This is a(n) _indirect_ way to go. Your friend wants to walk from 10th and Cedar through the park because it is faster and more _direct_ .

2. The sun causes water from lakes and oceans to _rise_ and form clouds in the sky. When the clouds are above mountains, the water _falls_ to the earth as rain. The falling water in mountain rivers is our source of hydroelectric energy.

3. a. Numbers are _infinite_ ; that is, if you want to count all the possible numbers, you will never stop because they continue forever. It is also possible to say that the numbers between 1 and 2 are _infinite_ . The number 1.236450628098436 is an example of one possible number between 1 and 2.

   b. Other things can be _finite_ . Let me give you an example. Natural resources such as oil, water, and wood are limited. In the future there will be much smaller amounts of these resources.

4. In the winter, the house is cold, and we use the _heating_ system. The opposite happens in the summer. During the warm months, some people use a(n) _cooling_ system. This makes the temperature in the house: a. rise   ⓑ. fall

5. There are different kinds of energy, but not many are _non poulluting_ . In large cities, fossil fuels pollute the air. Unfortunately, the majority of the energy sources today are _polluting_ .

6. He started to read at the _top_ of the page, but when he was at the _bottom_ of that page, he was asleep.

7. a. Water boils at 100 degrees centigrade at sea level. In the mountains, however, it boils at a lower temperature. This is a(n) _basic_ fact that people who live at high altitudes learn quickly because it takes longer to cook food.

b. A business executive is usually very busy and has many things to do every day. The life of a businessperson is ___complicated___. In contrast, someone who lives in the countryside may have a more ___basic___ lifestyle.

c. Heating a house with the sun is easy, but heating with electricity from nuclear power is more ___complicated___.

Part 2
Reading

Warm-Up Activity: Skimming

Skim the reading quickly for general ideas. Write numbers to show how each paragraph functions.

Paragraph Number	Paragraph Function
2	an introduction to a graphic
3	an extension of the main topic
4	a description of a process
1	general information on types of energy
5	a discussion of advantages and disadvantages

Does the reading move from general to specific (usual English organization)?

Discuss your answers with a partner.

HOME HEATING: SOLAR ENERGY

1 Most of the forms of energy that we use today come from sunlight. Plants provide energy for our bodies, and they get this energy from the sun. Fossil fuels (oil, natural gas, and coal) are forms of energy stored in the earth for millions of years, and these too come from plants and, indirectly, the sun. Wind and hydroelectric power are also indirect forms of energy from the sun. Nuclear power, in contrast, is not a form of solar energy. Because fossil fuels will not last indefinitely, research with alternative sources of energy must result in solutions to the world's energy problems.

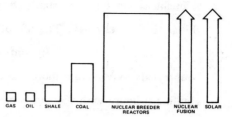

Figure 1. Potential U.S. Energy Resources.
Adapted from *Nuclear Power: Technology on Trial*
by James J. Duderstadt and Chichiro Kikuchi.
Copyright © 1979 by the University of Michigan
Press.

2   Unlike other sources of power, the sun provides an almost infinite supply of nonpolluting energy. See Figure 1. Energy from the sun falls on the United States, for example, at approximately 600 times the current rate of consumption. This will continue for billions of years. With solar energy, it is not necessary to burn fossil fuels in the air. Today the majority of our energy sources are fossil fuels, fuels that are in short supply and that pollute the environment. Nuclear energy is a finite source of energy, and its radioactive waste is destructive to the environment. Because of these problems, scientists are looking to solar energy.

3   Figure 2 shows a solar heated home with a Trombe wall made of rock. The purpose of the Trombe wall is to heat the house using the sun. The diagram illustrates the basic principles in solar home heating. This is a passive system; it requires no electric fans or other equipment.

4   During the winter, the sun is low in the sky. Sunlight goes through the glass wall on the south side of the house and shines on the Trombe wall. The sunlight then changes to heat energy and warms the air and the rock in the wall. The basic principle at work here is this: Hot air rises. The warmed air travels up through the top vent and enters the living area. At the same time, cool air from the living area goes through the bottom vent to replace the hot air now in the living area. After a while, the air in the living area is warmer. Many solar home heating systems include more complicated equipment, but the Trombe wall illustrates the basics.

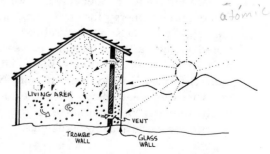

Figure 2. Trombe Wall: Daytime Use

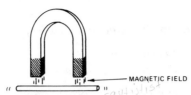

MAGNETIC FIELD

5   In addition to solar energy, scientists are interested in other types of alternative energy development. One type is nuclear fusion. Fusion is less dangerous than fission, the process used today. Nuclear fusion, like solar energy, has the potential to provide an inexhaustable energy supply. At present there are problems of containment: The process cannot be contained in a limited area. Superconductors are a second type of energy development that hold promise for the future. Superconductors do not involve energy production but do involve energy transport. With superconductors, it is possible to transport electricity much more efficiently than with electric wires, where much of the energy is lost. Large quantities of energy can be saved. Superconductors may also help with the development of fusion energy. The powerful magnetic field that superconductors create may be a way to contain the fusion process. With scientists and other researchers throughout the world working on energy alternatives such as solar heating, solar energy production, nuclear fusion, and more efficient transport, our children may live in a safer and less polluted world.

Part 3
Understanding Through Writing

General Comprehension

Write answers; then discuss your answers in small groups.

1. What form of energy development seems to you to be the best for the future? What have you read about alternative energy development lately? What recent progress has there been with superconductors?
2. Figure 2 describes a process. List the steps in the process in order.
3. Give four examples of forms of energy from sunlight in paragraph 1.
4. Read paragraph 2 again. The main idea is unstated, but facts direct the reader to the main idea. Answer these questions about the facts.
   a. What kind of energy does the sun provide?
   b. What kind of energy do we use today for the most part?
   c. Are fossil fuels polluting or nonpolluting? In infinite supply or in short supply?
   d. Is nuclear energy infinite or finite? Polluting or nonpolluting?
   e. Think about these facts. What is the main idea of the paragraph?

Word Study

Write words from the reading.

Location by Paragraph	Meaning	Word
1. end of 1	providing a choice	*alternative*
2. end of 2	giving off nuclear rays	destructive
3. middle of 3	drawing	diagram
4. 3	to give a picture of	illustrates
5. 3	general laws or truths	_____
6. end of 4	elementary or basic things	basics
7. 5	names of two nuclear processes	fusion fission
8. beginning of 5	infinite	_____
9. middle of 5	kept in a small area	_____

Sentence Study: Identifying Synonymous Sentences

Which sentences restate the first sentence? Circle the letter(s) of your choice(s).

Example: Most of the forms of energy that we use today come from sunlight.
   a. The sun provides enough energy for today's energy needs.
   ⓑ Sunlight provides the basis of much of the energy currently in use.
   ⓒ Sunlight is the source of the majority of energy types used today.

Choice *a* is not a good restatement; it says that the sun gives us enough energy for "today's energy needs." The first sentence says that most forms of energy in use come from the sun. Choices *b* and *c* are good restatements. The focus in both is on **most forms of energy in use now**. Both sentences say that the source of these energy forms is sunlight.

1. Unlike other sources of power, the sun provides an almost infinite supply of nonpolluting energy.
   a. Energy from the sun is similar to other energy sources because it is nonpolluting and will last for billions of years.
   b. In contrast to other energy sources, the sun is a very limited but nonpolluting source of energy.
   c. The sun, in contrast to other energy sources, provides nonpolluting energy that will last for billions of years.

2. Energy from the sun falls on the United States, for example, at approximately 600 times the current rate of consumption.
   a. About 600 times more solar energy falls on the United States than is used there today.
   b. The current rate of energy consumption in the United States is approximately 600 times the solar energy that falls there.
   c. The solar energy that falls on the United States is about 600 times the current rate in use there.
3. Wind and hydroelectric power are indirect forms of energy from the sun.
   a. Energy from wind and water comes from the sun indirectly.
   b. Both wind and hydroelectric energy result directly from the sun.
   c. The sun provides power because of the solar winds on the sun.
4. Plants provide energy for our bodies, and they get this energy from the sun.
   a. Plants grow with the help of solar energy; they, in turn, provide energy for humans.
   b. Plants and people receive their energy from the sun.
   c. The sun provides energy for plants; plants provide energy for humans.

Discourse Study: Sentence Reference

This/that and *these/those* can refer back to noun phrases:

There was a lot of important research last year. **That research** gives us more information so that work can continue.

That research = the large quantity of important research from last year

This and *that* can also refer back to a sentence:

Their heating bills are now lower because they have a solar hot water heater. **This** gives them a few extra dollars every month.

This = the fact that their heating bills are now lower because of the solar hot water heater

She had expensive solar panels put on the roof last year. **That** is why she is not making many home improvements this year.

That = the fact that she had expensive solar panels put on the roof last year

See the reading to answer.

1. See the second sentence of paragraph 1. What does *this energy* mean?

_____ nonpolluting energy that plants provide for our bodies

2. See the third sentence of paragraph 1. What does *these* mean?

_____fossil fuels, oil, gas, and coal_____

3. See the middle of paragraph 2. What does *this* mean in *This will continue for billions of years?*

_____the fact energy for the sun_____

Fill in the blanks.

4. This solar home heating system was designed by a solar architect. The architect designed several solar homes last year. **This** gave him valuable experience.

   This = the fact that _____
   (project)
5. There are lots of solar heated homes in this area. The reason for **this** is that we have a lot of sunshine during the winter months.
   situation
   This = the fact that ____lots_____
   Development

Part 4
Getting Ready to Write Paragraphs

The Present Tense

Review these common uses of the present tense:

Time	Type of Verb	Example
Habitual Action (usually, often)	Action (*go, come*)	She **leaves** for work early.
Current Time (now)	Stative (*think, like*)	He **wants** a new computer.

In academic writing, we find two other uses of present tense: general truths and a series of actions.

General Truths

These statements are timeless; a general principle or law of nature is always true:

   The sun **rises** in the east.
   Water **flows** downhill.
   Water **boils** at 100 degrees Celsius at sea level.
   An object dropped from a high building **falls** to the earth.
   The sun **radiates** light.

These words can also signal a statement that is generally true:

Many, Most, Usually:	**Many** forms of energy are expensive. **Most** currently used forms are polluting. Energy production **usually** implies pollution.
Plural Nouns:	**Sources** of energy in use today are limited. **Scientists** are working hard on **semiconductors**.
Noncount Nouns:	**Coal** is a natural substance. (Noncount nouns are singular. Other examples: energy, power, electricity, sunlight, air, oil, natural gas, equipment.)

A Series of Actions

A series of actions describes a process:

First she **takes** the butter and sugar and **mixes** them together. Then she **adds** the eggs, milk, flour, soda, and spices. She **bakes** these cookies for about ten minutes.

A fan is an electrically powered device that **moves** the air. The blades **move** quickly and **push** the air to the front of the fan. More air **comes** in the back to replace the air that **goes** through the fan.

RECOGNITION EXERCISE

See the reading on page 75 to answer.

1. Find the general truth about hot air in paragraph 4. Is this statement always true or often true?

   _____

2. Write an original example of a general truth.

   _____

3. In paragraph 4, a process is explained from beginning to end. Three time expressions help to guide the reader through the process. The first is *then*. Write the two other expressions.

   _____   _____

EXERCISE 1

*Describe the series of actions in the diagram. Use these verbs: **heat, rise, form, pass over, fall, return.** Work on a separate piece of paper.*

Example: heat ___The sun heats the water in the lake.___

EXERCISE 2

Write general truths about these topics on a separate piece of paper. Choose your own topics for 7 and 8.

Example: sunlight

___Sunlight falls on the earth in very large quantities.___

1. young people
2. parents
3. corporations
4. the sun
5. water
6. oil
7. ?
8. ?

Part 5
Writing Paragraphs

Warm-Up Activities: Paragraph Writing Guidelines, Description of a Process

> **A.** Check (✓) the sentences with correct information about writing paragraphs in English. Discuss your choices in pairs.
>
> _T_ 1. A paragraph often begins with a topic sentence.
>
> _T_ 2. The topic sentence states the main idea of the paragraph.
>
> _T_ 3. The topic sentence limits the discussion to a small topic.
>
> _F_ 4. The topic sentence is the most specific sentence in the paragraph.
>
> _F_ 5. The discussion gives general ideas about the topic.

<u>I</u> 6. After each example or detail is introduced, additional sentences discuss it more fully.

(sometimes)
is true <u>I</u> 7. A paragraph sometimes ends with a concluding sentence that restates the main idea of the paragraph.

B. *Below are diagrams of Trombe walls for day and night use. What source of heat radiates into the living area at night? Compare the two diagrams. Make a list of the differences.*

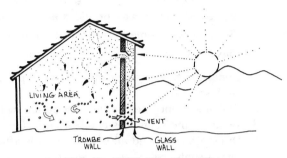

Trombe Wall: Daytime Use

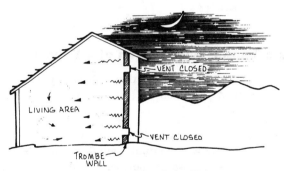

Trombe Wall: Night Use

Now read and discuss this description of the process at night:

The Trombe wall works differently at night, but it continues the process of heating a house. During daylight hours, sunlight shines on the south side of the house and heats the Trombe wall. The Trombe wall stores heat energy all day long. The residents close the top and bottom vents to begin the nighttime process. With both vents closed, the warm air does not excape so quickly. The sun does not now function as the source of heat because it is on the other side of the earth. The wall itself becomes the source of heat. A dense material such as rock retains heat for a long time. The heat from the rock wall radiates slowly into the living area and keeps the temperature from dropping off suddenly after sunset. The wall gives off most of its heat during the evening; the amount decreases during the late night hours. When the sun comes up again in the morning, the vents are opened, and the heating process begins again. Using a small fan at the top vent of the wall during the daytime greatly improves efficiency by moving the warm air. In areas with winter sunshine, a Trombe wall provides nonpolluting heat most of the time. This allows people to use heat from fossil fuels on only the coldest days of the year.

1. Underline the sentence in the paragraph that tells you a process will be described.
2. Which sentence begins the description of the nighttime process?
3. What do the sentences before that discuss? Are they necessary?
4. Draw a box around all the time words after *nighttime process* in the fourth sentence. How do these times help the reader?
5. Underline the verbs that describe the process.
6. Circle the general truth or principle about rock.
7. What facts about Trombe walls seem to be most important to the writer?

Choosing a Topic: Description of a Process

Choose a topic from these ideas or make up a process topic that interests you more. Choose a topic you know a little about or want to find out about.

— how hydroelectric (*or geothermal or wind*) energy works
— how a windmill (*wind-up clock, levitated train*) works
— how water cools land in the summer and heats it in the winter
— how a can opener (*microwave oven, bicycle, fireplace*) works
— how earthquakes happen
— how plants grow
— how inflation works
— how a researcher in your major field does research

Brainstorming for Ideas: Listing Steps in a Process

Brainstorm individually by listing the steps in the process. Read your list and make sure of the order. Then talk to a partner who is working on a similar topic. Exchange papers and discuss the steps in both processes. Is anything missing?

Work together on topic sentences for both paragraphs. Why is the process important? Is the process you are describing faster, easier, or better than another process? How does the process affect people's daily lives or well-being? How does it help people or society?

Writing a First Draft

Write the paragraph using the present tense. Tell each of the steps in the process in order. Include *this/that* or *these/those* for reference to things and ideas already mentioned. In your first draft, think about getting your ideas down on paper. You can work on spelling, punctuation, etc., later. After you finish, use the following checklist to edit your work. Make changes and copy the paragraph for your partner to read.

Checklist

1. What part of the paragraph do you like best? Why?
2. What process will be explained? Where do you learn this?
3. What is the importance of this process? Where is this stated?
4. Do all the sentences discuss the process and related ideas? Do you suggest adding or taking out anything?
5. What are the steps in the process? Is each one clear?
6. How does the writer end the paragraph? Do you have any other ideas?
7. Read the paragraph one time for grammar, including present tense for description of a process and clear use of *this/that* or *these/those* for reference. Read it a second time for punctuation and spelling.

Revising the First Draft

Read your partner's paper. Underline anything you have a question about. Use the checklist. Then discuss both papers together. Revise your paragraph based on your partner's suggestions.

CHAPTER SEVEN

Law

Law consists of the rules for a society and the ways that the society enforces its rules. Antitrust laws are for the specific purpose of preventing monopolies. In the United States, antitrust laws began in 1890 with the Sherman Antitrust Act.

No having laws
Lawlessness

organize of our lives
large society

Part ■
Vocabulary in Context

Content Vocabulary: Law

A. Read the paragraphs.

Blake and Rogers owned a used car company together. Blake worked hard, but Rogers often didn't even come to work although they were losing money. Blake told him several times, "We can't pay our bills. If you don't work harder, we will have to **file bankruptcy.**" Blake hoped that things might improve, but Rogers continued to do nothing. Blake decided he wanted to sell his half of the business, but Rogers refused to sell his half. Finally Blake decided to **sue** Rogers for $100,000. He decided that a **lawsuit** was the only way to get out of the situation.

Blake's lawyer prepared the arguments. He had this **evidence:** (1) Rogers seldom worked, (2) Blake's car sales were 15 times higher than Rogers', and (3) Rogers owed Blake money from the purchase of the business. In court, Blake's lawyer **accused** Rogers of these three things. The **jury** listened carefully; they **awarded** Blake the full $100,000.

B. *Write these words after their definitions.*

file bankruptcy ✓ lawsuit   accuse✓   award ✓
sue   evidence ✓   jury ✓

Example: a legal action ___*lawsuit*___

1. information that proves or disproves facts ___evidence___

2. bring a legal action against someone ___sue___

3. state that someone did something wrong or illegal ___accuse___

4. the people who listen to both sides of an argument in court and decide if someone is guilty of wrongdoing ___jury___

5. give, after judging the facts ___award___

6. ask for legal recognition that you can't pay debts ___bankruptcy___

Subtechnical Vocabulary: Parts of Speech

A. *Write letters in the blanks.*

  a. each business is trying to take customers from the others
✓ b. an action that is against the law
  c. a lot
  d. the only business of its kind in an area
  e. to discuss and reach a solution to a problem
  f. control
  g. a payment of money because of wrongdoing
  h. remove it

Example: When someone **violates** the law, this person breaks a rule. For example, if you drive your car at 40 miles per hour in an area where the speed limit is 25 miles per hour, this is a traffic **violation**.

A **violation** is ___*b*___.

1. When you **eliminate** something, you get rid of it or make it go away. The **elimination** of monopolies would mean no more monopolies.

To **eliminate** something is to ___h___.

2. Businesses **compete** against each other for customers. Sometimes business **competitors** will lower prices to try to increase sales.

If there is a lot of **competition**, ___a___.

3. One foggy morning last week I backed into a parked car. I admitted the accident was my fault, and we **settled** the problem quickly. I paid the owner of the car a **settlement** of $447.

   To settle a problem means ___e___. A **settlement** is _dispose of_

4. In the United States, liquor laws are **regulated** by each state. In some states, the **regulation** is not much, and a person can buy liquor any time. Other states **regulate** more, and a person can't buy liquor on Sunday, for example, or must go to a special state liquor store.

   When there is **regulation** of something, there is _control_

5. No other business in this part of town provides this service. The Copy Rite-N-Quik Company is a **monopoly**. The owners started a business with no competition and now **monopolize** the copying business in this area.

   If a business is a **monopoly**, it is ___d___.

6. There was a **drastic** change in the company's profits. Profits two years ago were $275,000,000, but last year they were only $156,750,000. The profits fell **drastically**—by 43%.

   If profits fall **drastically**, they fall _a lot._

B. *Write **noun**, **verb**, **adjective**, or **adverb** for each word.*

Word	Part of Speech
violate	*verb*
violation	noun
eliminate	verb
elimination	noun
compete	verb
competition	noun
settle	verb
settlement	noun
regulation	noun
regulate	verb
monopoly	noun
monopolize	verb
drastic	adj.
drastically	adv.

Part 2
Reading

Warm-Up Activity: Scanning

To scan is to read quickly for specific information.

Read these questions; then scan the reading for answers. (1 or 2 minutes)

1. Is monopolizing against the law in the United States?
2. Besides the Justice Department, what two small companies sued AT&T?
3. Who was the judge in the Justice Department case?
4. Is this reading numbered by paragraph or by line?

AMERICAN TELEPHONE AND TELEGRAPH:
A REGULATED MONOPOLY?

1   A *monopoly* is a business that sells a product or service with little or no competition from other businesses. When a company is a monopoly, it can make the price of its products high because no one else is selling the same thing. Monopolizing is a violation of U.S. law, but
5   sometimes the government will give monopoly power to a corporation. An example of this is American Telephone and Telegraph (AT&T), which was a monopoly regulated by the U.S. government until the early 1980s. During the period from 1974 to 1981, however, there were many lawsuits against AT&T. The U.S. Justice Department and
10   two of AT&T's competitors, among others, accused the company of monopolizing.

The Justice Department accused AT&T of monopoly practices: excluding competition in the telecommunications industry in the 1960s and 70s. There were 1,872 pages of evidence against AT&T. The
15   corporation's violations against two small companies, Datran and MCI Telecommunications, were a part of the Justice Department's lawsuit. These two companies also sued AT&T.

Datran developed a data transmission system in 1969; AT&T did not have the same kind of system then but created a similar system
20   soon afterward. AT&T then asked a low price for its competing system. This forced Datran out of business, and the company filed bankruptcy in 1976. In another example, the Federal Communications Commission authorized MCI to compete with AT&T for long-distance calls in 1978. MCI accused AT&T of delaying its progress and lower-
25   ing prices drastically in areas where the two companies competed for business.

As for the results in the Justice Department suit, the argument was settled out of court. Judge Harold Greene authorized AT&T to enter

William G. McGowan, Chairman and Chief Executive of MCI Telecommunications Corporation. Courtesy of MCI Telecommunications Corporation.

areas of telecommunications previously closed to it and required that
30 AT&T sell its 22 local telephone companies. Datran also settled its suit against AT&T outside the courtroom, accepting a $50,000,000 settlement from AT&T. The results of the MCI lawsuit were different. The Chicago jury awarded MCI $600,000,000, which, according to federal law, was tripled to $1.8 billion, the largest amount ever
35 awarded in an antitrust suit.

Part **3**
Understanding Through Writing

General Comprehension: Finding the Main Idea

Reread paragraphs 1, 3, and 4 to answer. Where there is a choice, circle one letter.

Paragraph 1

1. Before the 1980s, did the government give AT&T permission to be a monopoly or a regulated monopoly?

   _____ regulated monopoly _____

2. What happened to AT&T in the mid-1970s and early 1980s?

_____

3. Which of the following sentences expresses the main idea of the first paragraph?

   a. Monopolies are businesses that control the buying and selling of a particular product or service.

   b. The U.S. government regulated AT&T, but legal actions were taken against the company because some people thought the company was a true monopoly.

   c. AT&T was a regulated monopoly because the U.S. government gives only a small amount of power to corporations.

Paragraph 3

1. Why did Datran go out of business?

_____

2. What two accusations did MCI make against AT&T?

_____

_____

3. What was the probable result of AT&T's delays and low prices for MCI?

_____

4. The third paragraph doesn't have the main idea stated in one sentence. How does the paragraph function in the reading?

   a. It shows how competition can lower prices and help small businesses.

   b. It explains how AT&T helped competing businesses.

   c. It gives examples of AT&T's anticompetitive practices.

5. Write a topic sentence for the third paragraph.

_____

Paragraph 4

1. This paragraph discusses:

   a. arguments

   b. accusations

   c. results

2. The reader comes to a conclusion after reading the three examples. What conclusion did you come to? (Your answer will express the unstated main idea of the paragraph.)

_____

Word Study

Write words from the reading.

	Location by Paragraph	Meaning	Word
1.	beginning of 2	opposite of *include*	_exclude_
2.	beginning of 2	actions	_____
3.	end of 3	slowing down	*lowering prices*
4.	beginning of 4	gave permission	*settled out*
5.	end of 4	multiplied by three	*tripled*

Discourse Study

Reference to People and Things

Academic writing is not personal, so pronouns such as *I* and *you* are infrequent. The boxed pronouns are the most common:

Subject	Object	Possessive
I	me	mine
you	you	yours
she	her	hers
he	him	his
it	it	its
we	us	ours
you	you	yours
they	them	theirs

In academic papers, *I* and *we* mean the author(s): *I* for one author, *we* for more than one. *You* (meaning the reader) is rarely used.

Reminder:

it's = it is: The company is going to sue, but **it's** not going to win.
its = a possessive: I am sure the company will lose **its** lawsuit.

Reference to Time and Place

Then and *there* are common substitute words for time and place:

> In the early 1980s, many long distance companies began to compete with AT&T. MCI, Sprint, and other companies saw their shares of the long-distance market increase **then**.

then = in the early 1980s

Alexander Graham Bell, the inventor of the earliest telephone, was born in Edinburgh, Scotland. He moved from **there** as a child and lived most of his life in the United States.

there = Edinburgh, Scotland

EXERCISE 1

See the reading for the meaning of these expressions. Write their meanings according to the reading.

Examples: *it*, line 3 = <u>the company</u>

              its, line 3 = <u>the company's</u>

            this, line 6 = <u>the fact that the government sometimes gives</u>

                      <u>monopoly power to a corporation</u>

1. *the company*, line 10 = _____

2. *the corporation's*, line 15 = _____

3. *these two companies*, line 17 = _____

4. *then*, line 19 = _____

5. *its*, line 20 = _____

6. *this*, line 21 = _____

7. *the company*, line 21 = _____

8. *its*, line 24 = _____

9. *the two companies*, line 25 = _____

10. *it*, line 29 = _____

11. *its*, line 30 = _____

12. *its*, end of line 30 = _____

Part 4
Getting Ready to Write Paragraphs

Sequence Expressions

To narrate is to tell a story. Narration is telling actions or events in time order (sequence). The past tense is used for completed actions and is common in narrative writing and speech. Narration is used to tell what happened in a research experiment or study, for example. Narration of a past event can also help to prove a writer's point.

Sequence expressions show the order of events in narration. They help the reader to move through a piece of writing:

Ms. Sutcliffe bought a used car from Blake and Rogers. **A few weeks later**, she was hit from the rear, and the car caught fire. She was hospitalized for two weeks. As she lay in the hospital bed, she planned the legal action she wanted to take. **First**, she called her lawyer and talked about the case with him. She asked her lawyer for the name of a lawyer who specialized in auto accidents. **After that**, Ms. Sutcliffe talked at length with the new lawyer, and **in the end**, she decided to sue the automaker, not Blake and Rogers.

First Step:	first, first of all, to begin with
Second Step:	second, secondly
Other Steps:	then, next, after + noun (for example, after the test), after that, afterward, later, a year later, subsequently, at that time, at the same time
Last Step:	finally, in the end

All the expressions can come at the beginning or end of the sentence:

First of all, she checked with her lawyer.
She checked with her lawyer **first of all**.

After that, she got a second opinion from another lawyer.
She got a second opinion from another lawyer **after that**.

Then can come at the beginning, middle, or end of a sentence:

Then she filed a lawsuit against the automaker.
She filed a lawsuit against the automaker **then**.
She **then** filed a lawsuit against the automaker.

At the beginning, use a comma after all the expressions except *then*.

Reminder: For sequence, *then* means "next." *Then* is also used for times: "I go to work at 7:30. I'm always up an hour before **then** (= 7:30)."

Introducing Examples

Use these expressions when introducing examples:

for example	for one thing
for instance	to illustrate
to give an example	to give a specific instance

Most cities have several long-distance telephone companies. **For example**, there are six in the Boston area.   (OR)   There are six in the Boston area, **for example**.

An example of *X* is *Y*.
An example of a long-distance phone company is Sprint.

Y and *Z* are examples of *X*.
Sprint and MCI are examples of long-distance phone companies.

RECOGNITION EXERCISE

See the reading on page 89 to answer.

1. The third paragraph gives two long examples: One is about Datran and the other is about MCI. Both examples are narratives because they tell **what happened**. Which example has sequence expressions?

   _____

2. What are the two sequence expressions in this example?

   _____   _____

3. What other expressions in the same example help the reader to understand the time order? (*Look for specific time expressions.*)

   _____   _____

4. What does *then* mean in line 20 of the reading? _____

   _____

5. See the first paragraph. What is the example of a business to which the U.S. government gave monopoly power?

   _____

EXERCISE 2

Read and fill in the blanks. Choose from: **in the end, secondly, next, first of all, then, after that.**

Ms. Sutcliffe's lawyer went through a long process to research her case against the manufacturer of her car. (1) _first of all_, he looked at similar lawsuits. There had been three similar lawsuits the previous year. They all concerned the same problem in the same car, and all three had been settled out of court. (2) _secondly_, the lawyer interviewed the car owners in these cases and learned that they had received large amounts of money to settle out of court. (3) _after that_, the lawyer learned more about the safety record of the automaker and talked to more people with complaints. (4) _in the end_, he decided that there was a lot of evidence against the automaker.

EXERCISE 3

A. *Add a few sequence expressions to the second half of this paragraph. The first one is done as an example.*

Bob and Jim drove for quite a while before they found the perfect fishing spot. They walked along the river and came to a large pool of quiet water—the best place to find hungry fish looking for food. They set down their packs quietly. At the same time, Jim asked Bob to show him what to do. *First of all,* Bob showed Jim how to put together the pieces of his portable rod. *Secondly,* He put a larger hook on the end of his line. *After that* He put a worm on the hook. This was one part of fishing that he didn't enjoy. *Then* Jim watched Bob several times before he understood exactly how to throw out the line. He tried it himself. To his surprise, he caught a fish after only 10 minutes.

B. *Tell what Bob had to do to prepare for the trip. Write a paragraph to explain the list of actions as a narrative sequence. Use sequence expres-*

sions and expressions to introduce examples. Begin with: **Bob had to do a lot of things to get ready for the fishing trip.**

go with Jim to get fishing licenses
find his fishing equipment and raingear
buy some hooks at the sporting goods store
get a map from the Forest Service
make a lunch and pack up his equipment
dig up some worms for bait
get gas and pick up Jim

Part 5
Writing Paragraphs

Warm-Up Activity: Supporting a Thesis

Read the following paragraph. What is the thesis? How does the writer support it?

The purpose of the case against AT&T in the early 1980s was to break up a monopoly, but the results were more helpful to AT&T than if the corporation had actually stayed as it was. For one thing, the court ordered AT&T to sell its 22 local companies. Local telephone service is expensive to operate, and according to AT&T, the company had balanced these large expenses before the 1980s with its profitable long-distance service. The local companies became independent as a result of the case. Soon afterward, they raised their rates because local service had to pay for itself. Secondly, Judge Greene allowed AT&T to keep its long-distance service. According to a source at ITT, most cities in the United States now have at least five major long-distance companies and several smaller ones. So many companies are in competition for long-distance business today because it is very profitable. The third result of the case may prove to be the most important for AT&T: Large new markets were opened to the company. After the antitrust case, AT&T was free to enter the telecommunications industry and to develop computers and data processing equipment. This was among the fastest-growing areas of economic development in the United States at that time. In short, AT&T eliminated its unprofitable local service, kept its very profitable long-distance service, and then entered large new markets. These results surely pleased management at AT&T.

Answer on a separate piece of paper. Then discuss your answers in small groups.

1. Underline the thesis statement in the paragraph.
2. How many examples are used to support the thesis? Underline the words that tell the reader when a new example is introduced.
3. Are you convinced of the writer's thesis? Explain your answer.
4. Which of the examples in the paragraph are narratives? Circle the sequence expressions in the narrative examples.
5. What expression shows that the writer is summarizing the main points?
6. This material is a little long for one paragraph. Where could it be divided into two paragraphs?

Thesis: a position or a point assumed or made especially in controversy.

Supporting a Thesis

The topic sentence of a paragraph tells the writer's purpose. One purpose is to state an opinion (a thesis) that the writer tries to prove in the paragraph. A thesis is a general statement that the writer believes is true. The writer supports the thesis statement by using facts, statistics, or examples in the paragraph. If these details seem correct to the readers, they will probably believe the thesis statement. Here are some examples of thesis statements. Because they are generalizations, they are in the present tense:

(Writing 5)

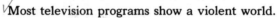

Most television programs show a violent world.
  People continue to wonder about the existence of life on other planets, but from my experience, UFOs definitely exist.
  A child's development depends more on peers than parents.
  California's temperate climate is healthy for most people.
  American students tend to spend more time and money on entertainment than international students do.

Think of two or three more thesis statements on topics of interest to you, and write them down. In small groups, read them aloud. Choose one statement and brainstorm together on ways to support it. How can you show that the statement is true? Think of as many facts, reasons, examples, or statistics as possible. Ask one person to take notes as the group works. When you're finished, share your results with another group or the class.

Choosing a Topic: Paragraphs of Argumentation

Choose a topic from these suggestions or from your group discussion.

1. Are there (regulated) monopolies in your country? Was there ever a lawsuit against this kind of business? Tell what happened in that court case (*or another trial of national or personal interest*). Begin the

paragraph with a thesis statement about the lawsuit and then prove your point: The case of (*company*) against (*company*) had positive results for the people of (*country*).   (OR)   In the lawsuit between (*country*) and (*company*), (*company's*) monopoly was broken up, which helped the people of (*country*) in several ways.

2. Are monopolies harmful? When can monopolies be helpful? Use a specific narrative example to prove your point. Begin with a thesis statement that tells your opinion about monopolies, multinational corporations, or a specific company. Use the rest of the paragraph to support that opinion.

3. Are there (dis)advantages to one form of energy? What experience or evidence makes you think this is true? Argue that one form of energy is more productive/efficient/destructive/wasteful than others.

4. What is a controversial topic of current interest?

5. Is there an issue in your field you can argue for or against?

6. Find a topic for which you can gather facts. For the following topics, for example, you could do an informal survey of 10 students in your class and 10 American students. Ask each person in both groups the same question: How much time do you spend studying on weeknights?   (OR)   How much time do you spend with friends every day? For your narrative example, tell how you got your results.

> On average, American students spend less time studying than international students do.   (OR)
>
> International students spend more time socializing with friends than American students do.   (OR?)

Getting Started

Brainstorm individually and then with a partner. Decide on your thesis first. Then think of as many ways as possible to support your thesis: facts and figures from authorities or your own experience. Write down your thesis statement and a list of supporting points. Include a narrative example of a past event to support your argument.

Check your notes. Remember that each point supports the thesis statement; your readers will want to know **why** your thesis is true. Show your notes to a partner. Ask for suggestions to make the argument stronger.

Writing and Editing a First Draft

Think only about getting the ideas on paper. Begin with your thesis statement, and keep it in mind as you write. Include the points from your notes. Use the past tense for the narrative example. Then edit your paragraph using the following checklist. Make changes and copy it for your partner.

Read your partner's paper, and underline anything you have a question about. Then discuss both papers together. Make any suggestions you can, and help your partner to rewrite anything that is not clear.

Checklist

1. Find a clear thesis statement in the present tense.
2. Are you convinced by the paragraph? Why or why not?
3. Find two or more ways that the writer supports the thesis.
4. Find a narrative example with sequence expressions. Is the order clear?
5. What, if anything, does not help the argument and should be removed?
6. For what point do you suggest giving more specific information?
7. Read the paragraph one time for grammar, including use of pronouns. Read it a second time for spelling and punctuation.

Revising the First Draft

Use your partner's suggestions to rewrite your paragraph. Make all the changes you want to, and copy it to hand in.

CHAPTER EIGHT

The Computerization of Air Travel

Computers are now in use in a variety of situations: industry, business, the sciences, the fine arts, engineering, education, and the home. Among the first industries to computerize were the international airlines. Today, even small businesses depend on computers to bill customers and to keep track of their merchandise.

Part 1
Reading

Warm-Up Activity: Skimming to Predict Content

Skim the reading quickly for main ideas; study the picture. Then check (✓) the topics you will probably learn more about when you read carefully.

_____ different types of airlines

_____ computerized airline reservation systems

_____ effects of the jet on air travel

_____ how the jet engine was developed

_____ increases in airline flights

_____ advantages of a flight to Europe for vacation

_____ effects of the computer on airline reservations

Return to this section after you read again. How well did you guess?

COMPUTERS IN THE AIR TRAVEL INDUSTRY

1   Years ago, it took several days to confirm reservations for international flights. Today international reservations are confirmed within seconds. The difference is the computer.

2   Computers have changed the way that industrialized nations do business. The "second generation" computers of the 1960s could process data much faster than the earlier machines. Computer experts began to talk in terms of *milliseconds* (1/1000 of a second) and *microseconds* (1/1,000,000 of a second) for computer operations. With fast and reliable information available, many uses of the computer became common. The development of computerized reservation systems for air travel was one of the first significant uses of computers in business. What were the reasons that led to the computerization of airline reservation systems? There were several, but the source of change was the invention of the jet engine.

3   With the development of the jet engine in the 1950s, air travel became faster. This had several effects on the air travel industry. First, more people took advantage of air travel. Travel by air saved time, so it became more popular with everyone from businesspeople to tourists. A related effect was an increase in the number of flights needed. From 1958 to 1968, the number of air passenger flights grew by 200%. A third result was an increase in the number of long-distance flights. Businesspeople began to take international flights regularly, and tourists began to fly to Europe for vacations. In summary, increases in the number of passengers, in the number of flights, and in the number of long-distance flights put pressure on the airlines for a reservation system that handled more information quickly.

4   The computer provided the solution. In 1968, 10 years after the jet age began, computer reservation systems in the United States handled 300 million reservations for 150 million airline passengers. International statistics were equally impressive. In 1968, the system at Air France, one of the first international airlines to computerize, could answer a question from any city tied into its reservation center in 8 seconds. The computer reduced the international reservation time from several days to several seconds. It answered the challenge of the jet age.

Part 2
Vocabulary Follow-Up

Subtechnical Vocabulary: Parts of Speech

A. *Check your understanding of words from the reading.*

1. "Hello, Worldwide Airlines? Can I get a seat on Flight 205 to London next Tuesday? And I need a return flight on the 23rd." "I can **confirm** a reservation for Tuesday at 9 a.m. **Confirmation** on the return trip is a problem, but I can put you on a wait list."

   a. Does the caller have a **confirmation** on the return flight?

   _____

   b. After a ticket agent **confirms** your reservation on a flight, do

   you have a reservation? _____

2. Quickbuck Loans, Inc. **computerized** its records last year. At first, the cost of **computerization** was high. The computer and employee training were expensive, but after the computer was working, there was a drastic cost **reduction**. The computer was less expensive than the manual system because it **reduced** the time necessary to do the work.

   a. What **computerized** service do you use? _____

   b. Which boldfaced word is the opposite of **increased?** _____

3. In many countries, governments are actively **developing** nuclear energy. However, some countries are active in solar research and **development**.

   a. What kind of energy are countries on your continent **developing?**

   _____

   b. Does **develop** mean "decrease" or "work with and improve"?

   _____

4. The new heavyweight boxing champion is Manny Marcus. Manny **challenged** last year's champion, Bruno, by calling him "a big wimp" on TV. Bruno had to take the **challenge** and fight. Manny won, but he knows there are many young fighters who see his win as a **challenge** to them.

   a. Do you want to climb Mount Everest or learn to scuba dive? Do you want to be a manager at your company or become a millionaire in 10 years? What is something that really **challenges** you?

   _____

b. Give an example of what a child might **challenge** another child to do.

_____

5. The young couple cooked a meal for 30 people, and the results were **impressive**. The beautiful meal certainly **impressed** the man's boss. She was surprised they cooked so well.

a. What **impressed** the man's boss? _____

b. When something is **impressive**, is it special or common? _____

_____

6. In the early 1970s, the government of Newcountry nationalized its mining industry. This was a **significant** step toward economic well-being for the people. No one thought it was a minor or unimportant decision. Its **significance** was clear.

a. Write the two antonyms (word opposites) for **significant**.

_____   _____

b. What is a **significant** event in recent history?

_____

B. *Write **noun, verb, adjective,** or **adverb** in each blank.*

Word	Part of Speech
confirm	_verb_
confirmation	_____
computerize	_____
computerization	_____
reduction	_____
reduce	_____
develop	_____
development	_____
challenge	_____ and _____
impressive	_____
impress	_____
significant	_____
significance	_____

Part 3
Understanding Through Reading and Writing

General Comprehension

Circle the best answer: a, b, or c.

1. A narrative tells a story. A description draws a picture in words of something or someone. A discussion of cause and effect gives causes and effects. Which describes the reading?
   a. a narrative
   b. a description
   c. a cause/effect discussion
2. Read the question in paragraph 2. Which statement is true?
   a. The writer does not know the answer to the question.
   b. The question does not give the topic of the reading.
   c. The answer to the question is a main idea in the reading.
3. The purpose of the question in paragraph 2 is to draw the reader's attention to a main idea. This type of question is called a *rhetorical* question. Where is the answer to the question?
   a. in the next sentence
   b. in paragraph 4
   c. understood, but not directly stated in any paragraph
4. The first sentence in paragraph 4 relates paragraph 4 to the rest of the reading. It mentions a solution. What problem does the solution solve?
   a. the computerization of reservation systems
   b. the demand for a reservation system that handled more information quickly
   c. the demands of businesspeople and tourists on international flights
5. The main idea of paragraph 4 is stated in the first sentence and again:
   a. in the second sentence
   b. in the third sentence
   c. in the last sentence

Word Study

Write words or phrases from the reading.

Location by Paragraph	Meaning	Word or Phrase
1. middle of 2	work done by computer	*computer operations*
2. middle of 2	accurate, dependable	_____
3. beginning of 3	use for your own benefit	_____
4. middle of 3	opposite of *cause*	_____

Location by Paragraph	Meaning	Word or Phrase
5. middle of 3	opposite of *cause*	_____
6. middle of 3	a traveler on airplanes	_____
7. end of 3	pushed, forced	_____
8. end of 3	took care of, processed	_____
9. beginning of 4	gave the answer	_____

Sentence Study: Identifying Synonymous Sentences

Read the first sentence. Circle a or b to complete the second sentence. The second sentence will restate the idea.

Example: Computers have changed the way that industrialized nations do business.

Industrialized countries conduct business differently today ...

　(a.) because of computers.
　b. because more information is available.

The first sentence says that the cause of change is the computer, not that there is now more information available.

1. The development of computerized reservation systems for air travel was one of the first significant uses of computers in business.

   Handling air travel reservations by computer was ...

   a. one of several major early uses of the computer for business.
   b. the first important use of computers in the area of business.

2. With the development of the jet engine in the 1950s, air travel became faster.

   Air travel took less time beginning in the 50s ...

   a. because there were new technological developments.
   b. because the jet engine was developed.

3. Travel by air saved time, so it became popular with everyone from businesspeople to tourists.

   People began to like air travel more ...

   a. because it took less time.
   b. because businesspeople and tourists wanted to take trips.

4. A third result was an increase in the number of long-distance flights.

   A third effect was that ...

   a. the flights went for longer distances.
   b. there were more long-distance flights.

Discourse Study: Clarity of Expression

There are expressions that help a writer to introduce a topic, list main ideas, and summarize them. These expressions show what the writer is doing in each part of a paper. They guide the reader through a piece of writing.

Introducing a Topic

There + *be* and present tense make general statements to introduce the main idea of a paragraph:

There were { several / three major / a number of } causes of the U.S. Civil War.

Economic problems sometimes **cause** wars.

Giving Main Points: Subject Signals

Adverbs such as *first of all, after that,* and *finally* introduce main points. The subjects of sentences can also introduce main points:

> There were several major causes of the Civil War in the United States. **One cause** was economic. The South was agricultural, and cheap slave labor helped to make farming profitable. **A second cause** was political. The North had the population and the political power to force laws on the South. Southerners did not like changes made in their way of life by strangers thousands of miles away.

In this example, the new points are causes. Using subject signals for different causes, reasons, or results makes writing easy to understand. Other examples: *the first effect, a second cause, a related effect, an additional result.*

Summarizing Main Points

At the end of a discussion, a writer often restates the same ideas quickly as a review for the reader. For example, the last sentence of the paragraph about the Civil War might read:

> **In summary**, the Civil War was fought not so much over slavery itself, but over related economic and political problems.

Other examples: *to summarize, in conclusion, briefly then, to review the facts, in other words, in short.*

See the reading at the beginning of this chapter to answer.

1. Find the sentence in paragraph 2 that introduces the specific points in paragraph 3. Write the complete sentence.

_____

_____

2. Write two subjects of sentences that signal new points in paragraph 3.

_____   _____

3. Write the summarizing expression in paragraph 3. _____

Part 4
Getting Ready to Write a Short Composition

People who travel a lot by airplane spend more time at a higher altitude. Because airlines generally fly at 35,000 feet or more, these people are exposed to greater radiation from the sun. Jet-setters are exposed to more radiation than other people, so researchers are investigating whether they may have higher rates of cancer.

— Why are air travelers exposed to greater amounts of radiation?
— What is a possible result of jet-setters being exposed to greater amounts of radiation?

This paragraph discusses causes (or reasons) and effects (or results). This is a common way to organize writing in English.

*Read these sentences and decide if each is a **cause** or an **effect**. Write C (cause) or E (effect) in the blanks. The first one is an example.*

1. _C_ The difference is the computer.

2. _____ The source of change was the invention of the jet engine.

3. _____ Air travel became faster.

4. _____ Travel by air saved time.

5. _____ It became more popular with everyone from businesspeople to tourists.

6. _____ A third result was an increase in long-distance flights.

7. _____ In 1968, the system at Air France could answer a question from any city tied into its reservation center in 8 seconds.

So and *Because*

So and *because* show a cause/effect relationship. *So* is a conjunction like *and, but*, and *or*. *So* introduces the result clause. *Because* introduces the cause or reason:

We can be in another part of the world in hours,
so some people say that the earth is "getting smaller." =

Some people say that the earth is "getting smaller" **because** we can be in another part of the world in hours.

The sentences mean the same. A comma comes before *so* but not before *because*. The clause with *because* can also come first. When it does, a comma is used:

Because air travel is fast, some say the earth is "getting smaller."

Note: For is a formal conjunction that is sometimes used to introduce a cause or reason: Think before you speak, **for** you cannot unsay a word.

Other Cause/Effect Sentences

X = the reason or cause; Y = the result or effect:

X causes Y.	Smoking causes heart disease.
X results in Y.	Smoking results in heart disease.
X leads to Y.	Smoking leads to heart disease.
X is one cause of Y.	Smoking is one cause of heart disease.
Y is caused by X.	Air pollution is caused by auto exhaust.
Y results from X.	Air pollution results from auto exhaust.
Y is the result of X.	Air pollution is the result of auto exhaust.
One effect of X is Y.	One effect of auto exhaust is air pollution.
X happened. As a result, Y occurred.	In the 1970s, researchers found that smoking was bad for health. As a result, many people stopped smoking.

When we say "X is the cause of Y," it means that X is the only cause. This is an absolute statement; there are no other possible causes. When there is only one cause, this is the right sentence to use. When there might be other explanations, the writer can show that there are other possible reasons, causes, or effects with sentences like these:

Smoking **can** cause lung cancer.
Lung cancer **sometimes** results from smoking.
Lung cancer is **one possible** result of smoking.
Lung cancer is caused **in part** by smoking.
Lung cancer is **one of several** effects of smoking.

EXERCISE 1

Read the question. On a separate piece of paper, combine the next two sentences with **so** + *result clause. Then rewrite each sentence using* **because**.

Example: This ticket is expensive. Why didn't you get a super-saver fare?

I wasn't able to get a special price.
I called only a week before the flight.

I called only a week before the flight, so I wasn't able to get a special price.

I wasn't able to get a special price because I called only a week before the flight.

1. Why are so many farmers filing bankruptcy these days?
   Many farmers are going out of business.
   Small farmers cannot compete with large-scale farming.

2. Why did data in the 70s show a reduction in the rate of heart disease?
   Research showed that smoking was a significant cause.
   Many people stopped smoking.

3. I'm confused. Why are there so many new techniques in language teaching?
   There is a lot of research in the field.
   Innovations in language teaching are common.

4. Why are so many libraries changing to computer systems?
   Libraries are computerizing.
   The huge amount of materials is impossible to handle manually.

5. We use fossil fuels in great quantity these days. How does this affect the supply of fossil fuels?
   It takes longer to create fossil fuels than to use them.
   They are in short supply these days.

EXERCISE 2

On a separate piece of paper, write sentences telling what these actions can result in. Give two different sentences for each item. Use every type of sentence in "Other Cause/Effect Sentences," page 109, at least one time. Do not write absolute statements.

Example: eating sugary foods

Eating sugary foods can result in poor nutrition.

Hyperactivity is a possible result of eating sugary foods.

1. frequent exposure to the sun
2. travel from one side of the world to the other
3. frequent reading without enough light
4. eating leftover meat that wasn't refrigerated
5. not getting enough sleep
6. increases in the number of women working outside the home

Part 5
Writing a Short Composition

Warm-Up Activity: Cause/Effect Thesis Statements

One type of thesis statement is a cause/effect statement. With a cause/effect thesis statement, the writer may try to prove that an event has a number of specific effects or causes. The thesis statement introduces the topic and tells whether its causes or effects will be discussed:

There were a number of causes of the recent economic recession.
Our decision to get a business computer had several positive effects.
The new marketing practices resulted in two immediate changes.
There were three major causes for his decision to quit his job.
Daily exercise affects both the body and the mind.

Note: The noun is *effect*; the verb is *affect.*

Make up two cause/effect thesis statements. Introduce effects of the computer on the airline industry in one or both of your sentences. Write down your thesis statements, and read them to a partner for discussion.

Getting Started

In this section, you will write a short composition of four paragraphs. Follow this outline for your paper. Decide on A, B, or C for paragraph 4:

Paragraph 1: the importance of computers in everyday life
Paragraph 2: the development of the computer
Paragraph 3: the effects of computers on the airline industry
Paragraph 4: A. restatement of the importance of computers (OR)
              B. possible future uses of computers (OR)
              C. cause and effect chain: A causes B, which results in C. C, in turn, can lead to D, and D may result in E.

Example:

computers make international travel easier

↓

larger numbers of people go to foreign countries

↓

greater understanding of other peoples

↓

better international relations between countries

↓

?

Gathering Information

Use information from these notes for the first, second, and third paragraphs of your paper. Begin by discussing the notes in small groups. Ask about anything you don't understand. Then study the notes and think about which points to include. It is impossible to discuss them all in a short composition, so choose a few items for each paragraph.

Everyday Uses of Computers

cameras	calculators
photocopiers	typewriters
cars (ignition, fuel injection)	automated teller machines
traffic lights	medical equipment
supermarket checkout scanners	business communications
digital watches	figuring and writing paychecks
microwave ovens	word processing
televisions	VCRs

Cray X-MP Supercomputer.
Photo courtesy of Cray Research,
Inc.

Development of the Computer

1876: Lord Kelvin (England) built an analog machine: quick, but not very accurate. Used in physics and engineering.

1890: Herman Hollerith (U.S.) developed a machine using punch cards. In 1896, he formed the Tabulating Machine Company, which later became International Business Machines Corporation (IBM).

1937: Howard H. Aiken (U.S.) designed the automatic digital computer. Weight: 5 tons. Computing speed: 6 seconds per multiplication.

1945: Eckert, Mauchly, Goldstine, and Brainerd (U.S.) developed ENIAC (Electronic Numerical Integrator and Computer). Computing speed: 300 multiplications per second.

1947: Bell Labs (part of AT&T) developed transistors. In the late 1950s, computers with transistors were developed. Computing speed: multiplication of two 10-digit numbers in 1/100,000 of a second.

1960s: Computers helped design "second-generation" computers.

1970s: Microcomputers were developed using solid-state memory and tiny silicon chips. Cray Research became a leader in the production of supercomputers like the Cray 1.

1980s: Cray Research developed the Cray 2 and the Cray X-MP computers. Computing speed: nanoseconds (billionths of a second). Computers became so complicated that computer-aided design (CAD) became a critical tool in their design.

Effects of Computers on the Airline Industry

quick reservations
safe landing of many jets; safe landing in bad weather
quick payments, seating, estimated arrival times
help in design and manufacture of jets
weather prediction using data from satellites

Getting Organized

Write down organizational ideas for your composition. Use the paragraph outline in "Getting Started," (page 111), and add a limited amount of specific information from the notes and your own knowledge. Write a topic sentence or thesis statement for each paragraph.

In pairs, tell what you plan to discuss in each paragraph. Ask your partner to look at your topic sentences to see if they are clear. Make sure that your partner is not trying to discuss too many ideas. Offer any suggestions you have.

Writing a First Draft

Concentrate on getting your ideas down on paper. Follow your outline, and work one paragraph at a time. Use the topic sentences or thesis statements that you wrote for each paragraph. Try to write all four paragraphs in one sitting. After you finish, read your paper carefully and use the following checklist. Make all changes, and copy the composition for your partner to read.

Checklist

1. What do you like best about this composition? Why?
2. What is the purpose of each paragraph? Find a clear statement of the writer's thesis or topic for each.
3. Find subject signals and expressions like *first of all* in the second paragraph. Is the order clear?
4. Find the sentences that introduce effects in paragraph 3. Is it clear when discussion of one effect stops and the next one starts?
5. Is the discussion in paragraph 3 convincing? Why or why not?
6. Is there anything in paragraph 3 that you suggest adding or removing because it doesn't help to prove the cause/effect thesis?
7. In the last paragraph, does the writer restate ideas or discuss something a little different? Find one or more sentences that relate the last paragraph to the rest of the composition.
8. Read the paper once for grammar and again for spelling and punctuation.

Revising the First Draft

Exchange papers with your partner for comments and suggestions. Use the checklist to go through your partner's paper. Underline anything that you have a question about. Then discuss both papers together. Help especially with restating any sentences that aren't clear. After your discussion, rewrite your paper according to your partner's most important suggestions.

CHAPTER NINE

Fast-Food Restaurants

During the last few decades, there has been huge growth in restaurants that specialize in fast food. If you don't have time to sit down for lunch, you can use the drive-through window and receive a hot meal in minutes to take back to the office. Fast food is popular with families because the prices are low and the service is fast. Today, over half of the U.S. population can drive to a McDonald's restaurant within three minutes.

Part 1
Vocabulary in Context

Subtechnical Vocabulary

*Underline the words with about the same meaning as the words in **boldface**.*

Example: Fast-food restaurants have been growing rapidly for **decades**. During the last ten-year period, many new restaurants started.

1. Ray Kroc is the **entrepreneur** who began McDonald's Corporation in the mid-50s. This businessman earned a billion dollars in a few years.
2. Kroc spent a **considerable** amount of time doing other work before he started the McDonald's Corporation. For example, he spent a lot of time selling paper cups and milkshake machines.

3. **In large part**, Kroc's success resulted from his good ideas and hard work. Good business sense was also important, but mostly it was his original idea and his constant work.
4. McDonald's restaurants have experienced **phenomenal** success. In their first 30 years of business, the restaurants sold over 50 billion hamburgers, an extraordinary number.
5. One **factor** in the success of McDonald's is the consistent quality of its product. Whether you buy a hamburger in Toronto or Tokyo, the quality is the same. This is one probable cause for the growth of McDonald's restaurants.
6. **Due to** the growth of McDonald's, other hamburger chains were started. Burger King and Wendy's are two examples of more recent chains. It may be because of the success of fast-food restaurants like these that many others are in business today.
7. Pizza Hut, Jack in the Box, Skipper's, and Long John Silver's are fast-food restaurants. The **latter** two specialize in seafood. The restaurants mentioned second are more recent than the ones mentioned first.
8. In addition to giving quick service, fast-food restaurants provide inexpensive meals. They can serve people quickly **as well as** cheaply.
9. Restaurant chains make a lot of money. Their **earnings** since the 1950s have been phenomenal.

Part ② Reading

Warm-Up Activity: Scanning

Scan the reading for the answers. (1 to 2 minutes)

1. How many women in the United States between the ages of 25 and 54 work?
2. What were McDonald's sales in 1987?
3. What two other fast-food places specialize in hamburgers?
4. Approximately how many fast-food restaurants are there today?

THE FAST-FOOD INDUSTRY IN THE UNITED STATES

1   For several decades, the fast-food industry in the United States has experienced phenomenal growth. Fast-food restaurants began in the early 50s; today there is one fast-food restaurant for every 685 people in the country. Experts estimate, for example, that more people worldwide eat at McDonald's daily than live in Australia and New Zealand. McDonald's sells burgers at the rate of 140 per second. The expansion and big earnings of these restaurants are in large part due to changes in the life styles of Americans.

2   One of the reasons for the growth is related to the fact that in the United States, more than seven out of ten women aged 25 to 54 now work outside the home. Nearly 80% of them are employed full-time. There is more money to spend on eating out and less time to prepare meals. Another reason is related to the huge increase in the 1970s and 80s in the number of people living alone. Singles as well as working mothers and their families find eating at fast-food restaurants quick, easy, and inexpensive. An additional factor is the increase in the use of the automobile on freeways for commuting, shopping, and recreation. The McDonald's or Burger King at freeway exits is a familiar landmark that represents consistent quality and service.

3   McDonald's, which specializes in hamburgers, is the largest restaurant chain, with over 10,000 locations worldwide. The company's sales in 1987 were $14.3 billion. A new McDonald's restaurant opens its doors every 17 hours. In urban areas of the United States, there is approximately one McDonald's for every 25,000 people, so estimating the population of a city is as easy as counting the number of McDonald's outlets in the city's telephone book. Burger King and Wendy's also specialize in hamburgers and have considerable sales. These latter two provide a great deal of competition for McDonald's famous Big Mac. Other companies that compete for the fast-food dollar are Kentucky Fried Chicken, Arby's Roast Beef, Hardee's, and Pizza Hut, to name only a few. Altogether, the fast-food industry sells over $100 billion worth of food a year.

4   In 1971, there were about 30,000 fast-food restaurants. Today there are more than 140,000. The existing restaurants are diversifying their menus, and new chains are still being created. Japanese entrepreneurs are particularly interested in the U.S. appetite for fast-food and are experimenting with noodle shops, fast sushi, and beef bowl restaurants. Fast-food chains are selling more healthful foods today. Salad bars are now popular, and some restaurants have beefed up sales by reducing the animal fat and salt in their products. The U.S. Bureau of Labor Statistics expects women's employment to rise in the 1990s and beyond. With most women on the job, fast-food chains will probably continue to profit from the change in life style.

Part 3
Vocabulary Follow-Up

Parts of Speech

*Check your understanding of these words. Circle a or b. Then tell the part of speech of each **boldfaced** word: noun, verb, adjective, or adverb.*

1. **Expansion** is important to the fast-food industry. McDonald's now finds it hard to **expand** in the United States because it already has so many restaurants, but it is **expanding** quickly in other areas of the world.

   To **expand** means: a. to make larger
                          b. to keep the same size as before

2. Fast-food restaurants **experiment** with new menu items to see if people like them. McDonald's **experiment** with breakfast sandwiches was tremendously successful.

   When you **experiment**, you: a. know exactly what will happen
                                 b. don't know exactly what will happen

3. McDonald's early success may be because of its **specialization** in hamburgers. It was cheaper and faster to prepare only one type of meal. Because the restaurant **specialized** in one thing, the workers could do it efficiently.

   To **specialize** means: a. to do only one thing
                            b. to do many different things, one at a time

4. The McDonald's Corporation **created** Hamburger University to train its employees. The **creation** of this training program helps McDonald's to control quality. It has become America's largest job training program.

   When you **create**, you: a. train someone for work
                          b. cause something to exist

5. Many of the oil-producing countries are **diversifying** their production. With **diversification**, these countries will not depend on one principal product but will be manufacturing many products.

   To **diversify** production means:
   a. to have one product for sale in large quantities
   b. to have a variety of products for sale

6. In many countries of the world, this sign **represents** "NO PARKING." The sign is an easy way to indicate areas where parking isn't allowed. This **representation** is clear without using words.

   To **represent** something is to:
   a. give a symbol of it, often without words
   b. say that you can't park it here, no matter what words you use

7. Often a teenager does not want to take his parents' advice but instead wants to learn by **experiencing** things and doing things for himself or herself. Learning by **experience** is something we all do.

   Experience means:
      a. knowledge or skill you get by doing things for yourself
      b. help from family or friends when a person has problems

8. Some states have laws requiring that repairpeople give written **estimates** for work done on cars. When repairpeople **estimate** the costs, the amount should be as close as possible to the amount they will charge.

   When you **estimate**, you give: a. the exact amount, size, quantity, etc.
                                     b. the approximate amount, size, etc.

9. My friend **commutes** into Los Angeles every day for work. It is a long drive, but she says that she doesn't like living in the city. For her, an hour's **commute** is OK.

   A person who **commutes**:
      a. takes a bus, train, or car to and from work every day
      b. doesn't like driving in the city

Part 4
Understanding Through Writing

General Comprehension

Answer about the reading.

1. How does paragraph 1 function in the reading? (*Circle two choices.*)
   a. introduces the topic of the reading
   b. gives examples of a variety of fast-food restaurants
   c. gives a sentence to lead into the topic of the next paragraph

2. What thesis does paragraph 2 support? (*Circle one choice.*)
   a. A large number of women in the U.S. now work outside the home.
   b. Fast-food restaurants are fast, easy, and inexpensive.
   c. Changes in life styles have led to growth in the fast-food industry.

3. Write the three expressions in paragraph 2 that introduce reasons.

   _____ _____ _____

4. How does paragraph 3 function in the reading? (*Circle two choices.*)

    a. gives examples of the phenomenal success of McDonald's restaurants

    b. gives specific examples of fast-food restaurants

    c. gives advice on where the best hamburger is available

5. What does the final paragraph discuss? (*Circle two choices.*)

    a. change and innovation in the fast-food industry

    b. importance of diversifying menus in the fast-food industry

    c. growth in the fast-food industry

Word Study

Write words from the reading.

Location by Paragraph	Meaning	Word
1. middle of 1	every day	*daily*
2. middle of 2	unmarried people	_____
3. end of 2	added, more	_____
4. end of 2	probable cause	_____
5. middle of 3	in the city, metropolitan	_____
6. beginning of 4	being here today	_____
7. middle of 4	hunger, desire for	_____
8. middle of 4	increased	_____

Sentence Study: Identifying Synonymous Sentences

Read the first sentence. Circle the best restatement of the first sentence: a, b, or c. Watch for sentences which are true but not good restatements. Discuss your answers in small groups and/or as a class.

Example: One of the reasons for the growth of the fast-food industry is related to the fact that over 70% of women aged 25 to 54 now work outside the home.

    a. The fast-food industry has grown because most women aged 25 to 54 work outside the home.

    b. The fact that over 70% of the women aged 25 to 54 work in the fast-food industry has contributed to its growth.

    c. The fact that over 70% of the women aged 25 to 54 now work outside the home is a contributing factor in the growth of the fast-food industry.

Choice *a* says the growth results from the fact that many American women work. The first sentence, however, says this is only one of the reasons.

Choice *b* says over 70% of the women aged 25 to 54 work in the fast-food industry. This is impossible. Choice *c* correctly points to working women as one of several factors ("a contributing factor") in the growth.

1. The expansion and big earnings of these restaurants are in large part due to changes in the life styles of Americans.
   a. The success of fast-food restaurants is principally caused by changes in American life styles.
   b. American life styles have caused a few minor changes in the fast-food industry.
   c. The success of fast-food restaurants is resulting in Americans making big changes in their life styles.

2. Another reason for the growth of the fast-food industry is related to the huge increase in the 1970s and 80s in the number of people living alone.
   a. The huge increases in numbers of people living alone is the major factor in the growth of the fast-food industry.
   b. Because of the huge increases in the fast-food industry, large numbers of people are living alone.
   c. The number of people living alone also contributes to growth in the fast-food industry.

3. There is approximately one McDonald's for every 25,000 people in urban areas.
   a. The number of urban McDonald's restaurants is decided by the population outside the city: one for every 25,000.
   b. In metropolitan areas, we find about one McDonald's restaurant for every 25,000 people.
   c. The planners for McDonald's decided that there should be one restaurant for every 25,000 people in the United States.

4. Japanese entrepreneurs are particularly interested in the American appetite for fast food and are experimenting with noodle shops, fast sushi, and beef bowl restaurants.
   a. Japanese businessmen know Americans like fast food and are trying various kinds of Japanese style fast-food restaurants.
   b. Japanese entrepreneurs eat more fast food than Americans because there are now noodle shops, fast sushi, and beef bowl restaurants.
   c. Americans have a big appetite for fast food and are now eating various kinds of Japanese fast food.

Discourse Study: Quantity Expressions and Numbers for Reference

Quantity expressions and numbers can refer back to noun phrases:

> In the early 1970s, there were about 30,000 fast-food restaurants. Today there are **140,000**.

> **140,000** = 140,000 fast-food restaurants

Other fast-food chains are Kentucky Fried Chicken, Arby's Roast Beef, Hardee's, and Long John Silver's, to name **a few**.

a few = a few other fast-food chains

*Write a second sentence using a quantity expression or number. Refer back to the noun in **boldface**.*

Example: In the past, **some fast-food restaurants** had mostly fattening foods.

  To provide less fattening foods, some now offer salads. (OR)

  Many are changing their menus due to customer demand.

1. Last year we had **ten different kinds of fast-food restaurants** here.

   _____

2. **Most of the fast food restaurants in this area** have hamburgers.

   _____

3. I like **several choices** at the fast-food place around the corner.

   _____

4. **Fast-food restaurants** are one result of a fast-paced life style.

   _____

Part 5
Getting Ready to Write Paragraphs

Nouns That Are Count and Noncount

Some nouns have one meaning as a **count** noun and a second meaning as a **noncount** noun:

Count Use: A CHANGE means "a difference, something new."
Noncount Use: CHANGE means "coins, metal money."

He needs **a change**. I hope he takes a vacation soon.
Do you need **change** for the phone?

Read the definitions and examples. The nouns in the examples are in mixed order. Decide on their meanings:

A PLAY = "live drama that you see at a theater"
  PLAY = "what people do for entertainment, recreation, or fun"

The children had a wonderful afternoon of **play**.
She saw an amusing **play** when she was in New York.

A COMPANY = "a business, a commercial enterprise"
COMPANY = (1) "companionship," or (2) "guests"

He is excellent **company**. (He is fun to be with.)
They often have a lot of **company** at their house.
We are starting a new **company** to design computer games.

A BUSINESS = "a shop or other commercial enterprise"
BUSINESS = (1) "buying and selling in general," or (2) "right"

He did **business** with my father for forty years.
They have a **business** on Pearl Street. It's a T-shirt shop.
You have no **business** asking me about that!

A QUALITY = "a characteristic or distinguishing feature"
QUALITY = "level of excellence or worth"

One of the **qualities** I especially like is the way she helps others.
Swiss watches are of exceptionally fine **quality**.

A SERVICE = "something done to help someone else"
SERVICE = "the serving of food and drink at restaurants, bars, hotels"

She did me a great **service** by helping me pass calculus.
The food at that restaurant is great, but the **service** is terrible.

A TIME = "an occasion, a particular afternoon, day, week, etc."
TIME = "the past, present, and future"

We have all the **time** in the world.
This **time**, I want to do it right. I've done it wrong two **times**.

A PAPER = (1) "a newspaper," or (2) "an essay, a composition"
PAPERS = "personal identification (passport, birth certificate, etc.)"
PAPER = "a substance made from wood used for writing, drawing, etc."

One student wrote a **paper** in only two weeks.
I need to get some **paper** at the office supply store.
You will need your **papers** when cashing a check at a foreign bank.
She went out before breakfast and got a **paper**.

Quantity Expressions

Expression	Used With
a great deal of	noncount noun
a great number of	count nouns

We can also say a **good** deal of and a **good** number of. Great and good both suggest "a lot," but a great number is more than a good number.

There is **a good deal of competition** between the two restaurants.
A great deal of the competition was started by the employees.
A good number of people came to my company's art show.
A great number of the people who came were dressed formally.

Pre-Articles with Fractions and Percentages

Count and noncount nouns are more exact with fractions and percentages:

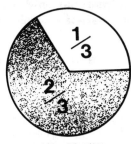

1/3 = 33-1/3%
2/3 = 66-2/3%

Two-thirds of the meat was spoiled.
Over 66% of the meat was thrown out.
Almost 3 out of 8 working hours today were wasted handling the
problem.

RECOGNITION EXERCISE

See the reading on page 116 to complete these statements.

Examples: ___Quality___ and ___service___ are the two nouns at the end of par-

agraph 2 that can be used as both count and noncount nouns. In the

reading, the nouns are used as ___noncount nouns.___
(count nouns/noncount nouns)

1. _____ is the quantity expression used in the middle of par-

agraph 3 with *competition* to indicate "a large quantity." This expression is used

only with _____; for that reason, *competition* must
(count nouns/noncount nouns)

be _____.
(count/noncount)

2. _____ is another noun that has count and noncount mean-

ings; it is used toward the end of paragraph 3 to mean "businesses." In the

reading, the noun is _____.
count/noncount

3. In paragraph 2 there is a fact about working women in the United States. A pre-article with a fraction is used to present this fact. Write the pre-article.

_____

4. The fact that many women in the United States now work outside the home is _____ for the growth of fast-food.
   (one of the reasons/several of the reasons)

EXERCISE 1

Fill in the blanks with **change, play, company, business, quality, service, time,** or **paper**. The context shows if the noun should be count or noncount.

> _Examples:_ Another name for a business is _____*a company*_____.
>
> This item isn't very good _____*quality*_____. I think I'll go to
>
> another store.

1. This morning I got _____ because I wanted to find out what was happening in the world.

2. I enjoy the theater. Next time we're here, let's see _____.

3. _____ of diamonds is that they are extremely hard.

4. She often has visitors and guests. In fact, I think she has _____ this week.

5. How many _____ did he tell you not to play with the cat?

6. There is usually excellent food and _____ at that restaurant.

7. He has no _____ asking you a question like that.

8. I'll need _____ for the parking meters when I go downtown.

EXERCISE 2

Write original sentences with **a great (good) number of** and **a great (good) deal of** + the nouns given. Use a separate piece of paper.

> _Examples:_ chocolate _A great deal of chocolate comes from Switzerland._
>
> classmates _A good number of my classmates speak English_
>
> _well._

1. land	5. films
2. work	6. gasoline
3. people	7. friends
4. natural resources	8. companies

Part 6
Using Suffixes

Suffixes are word endings. Suffixes change the part of speech of the words to which they are added. With *-ation*, *-tion*, or *-sion* + verb, the resulting word is a noun. See the minor spelling differences in some words:

Verb	*Noun*
expand	expansion
specialize	specialization
diversify	diversification
represent	representation
create	creation

Some nouns and verbs have the same form:

Verb	*Noun*
experiment	experiment
experience	experience
estimate	estimate
commute	commute

EXERCISE 3

Write words from the preceding lists. Each item will have a noun and a verb form of one word.

> *Examples:* Before Gary began medical school, he decided that pediatrics was
>
> going to be his ___*specialization*___. His love for children and babies
>
> made this an easy choice. Most of the people he knew during his
>
> school years also ___*specialized*___ in pediatrics.

1. Bob _____ to work. He lives an hour away by bus. He

   can read on the bus, so he says that the _____ isn't bad.

2. Betty invested all her money in land. People told her to _____

   and buy into business too. The area became unpopular because of a new air-

   port, and she lost lots of money. She had no _____ in her

   investments.

3. The imported food store was so popular that the owners decided to

   _____ their business and open a second store with the

same foods. They were doing so well, this _____ seemed smart.

4. My dictionary uses this kind of _____ for the sounds of words: /dɪkšənɛri/. You have to look at the bottom of the dictionary page to see what sound each of these symbols _____.

5. A scientist _____ with many combinations before discovering something. The ability to think creatively helps to make a(n) _____ _____ successful because it allows for unusual combinations.

6. Let's try to guess the approximate amount of money that we'll spend on the trip. I _____ that we'll spend about $200 for food and gas. Maybe it will cost more. What's your _____?

7. Kathleen learned a lot during her trip to the Middle East. She _____ _____ many things for the first time. These _____ helped her to understand different cultures.

8. In times of high unemployment, a lot of people don't have work. This situation _____ problems: People can't buy food and other basic necessities. Often the government can help by the _____ of additional jobs.

Part **7**
Writing Paragraphs

Warm-Up Activity: Discussion Questions

Discuss these topics in small groups. Take notes on topics of interest.

1. Opening a chain of fast-food restaurants makes excellent business sense today. Argue for and against this idea.
2. Do you eat out much? When you do eat out, do you choose fast-food restaurants? Why or why not? Which fast-food restaurants do you like the best? Why?
3. What agricultural products does your country grow? What products are manufactured in your country? Which products are most important to the people of your country? Which are exported?

Getting Started: Paragraphs of Argumentation

Choose a topic from the ideas that came up during your small group discussion. If you prefer, write about another idea that you can argue for or against. Write some organizational notes including a thesis statement for your paragraph. Your readers will want to know why the statement is true, so include as much support of the thesis statement as possible. For the third topic, see an encyclopedia or almanac at the library for additional information and statistics to support your thesis.

Show your notes and thesis statement to a partner for discussion. Ask your partner for one additional idea to support your thesis. Give your partner any ideas you have.

Writing a First Draft

Start with your thesis statement and/or with a fact that the reader should know at the beginning. Continue by getting your supporting ideas down on paper. Use subject signals (*an additional reason*) and/or sequence expressions (*first of all, secondly,* etc.) to introduce reasons. Then give one or two more sentences that explain each reason. Somewhere in your paragraph, use a number or quantity expression to refer back to a noun. Finish the paragraph with a concluding statement that begins with *to summarize, in short,* etc.

Read your paper all the way through. Use the following checklist to edit your paper. Then make the changes you want to, and copy it for a partner to read.

Checklist

1. Find a clear statement of the writer's thesis.
2. Is the thesis convincing? Why or why not?
3. Is there anything that you suggest adding to support the thesis or removing because it doesn't help to support the thesis?
4. Find the places where the writer guides the reader through the material (subject signals, sequence expressions, and summary statement).
5. Find a clear use of a number or quantity expression to refer back to a noun phrase. Are there any other places where you suggest using a pronoun instead of repeating a noun?
6. Read the paragraph one time for grammar. Then read it again for spelling and punctuation.

Revising the First Draft

Exchange papers with your partner for comments and suggestions. Use the checklist to go over your partner's paper. Underline anything that isn't clear. Then discuss both paragraphs. Help your partner to rewrite any unclear sentences. Rewrite your paragraph using your partner's most important suggestions.

CHAPTER TEN

Banking

In some countries, there are one or two central banks that handle the banking needs of the country. In other countries, there are many banks, all with different rules and regulations. The banks in the United States are all regulated by federal law.

Part 1
Vocabulary in Context

Content Vocabulary: Banking

*Answer about the words in **boldface**. When there is a choice, circle a or b.*

1. **Commercial banks** are sometimes called full-service banks because they offer a variety of services. Citibank, Bank of America, and Chase Manhattan are the three largest **commercial banks** in the United States.

   Write another example of a **commercial bank**. _____

2. According to U.S. law, most banks cannot establish **branches** in other states. In other words, they can expand in their own state only. They cannot **branch** across state lines.

   How many **branches** of your bank do you find in the Yellow Pages under "Banks"? Write the name of your bank and the number of **branches**.

   _____

3. **Interest** is money paid for the use of money. When you have a savings account, the bank pays you **interest;** when you take out a loan, you pay the bank **interest**.

   What is the **interest** rate on savings accounts in your country? __%

4. Most banks pay interest on savings accounts **quarterly**; that is, they pay interest four times a year.

   This bank pays interest **quarterly**. The first two payments this year were in March and June. In which months will the last two payments be made?

   _____   _____

5. The money in a savings account **earns** interest. You receive money because the bank can use your money while it is in the bank.

   What happens to the amount of money in an account that **earns** interest?
   a. It increases.
   b. It decreases.

6. A **balance** is the amount of money in a bank account. Some banks provide free checking when you keep a minimum **balance** in your account. This minimum **balance** requirement varies from $500 to $2000 or more.

   In a checking account, your **balance** represents:
   a. the amount of money you wrote checks for.
   b. the amount of money you didn't write checks for.

7. How often does your bank **compound** interest? If it **compounds** interest quarterly, interest is added to your balance every three months. Then you begin to earn interest on the total. When interest is **compounded** frequently, you earn more.

   Which kind of account earns more interest?
   a. an account for which interest is **compounded** daily
   b. an account for which interest is **compounded** quarterly

8. After you write a check, it goes from the store to the store's bank and then to your bank. The check **clears** after the bank makes sure you have enough money in your account to cover the amount of the check.

   When a check **clears**, this means there was:
   a. enough money in your account.
   b. not enough money in your account.

9. **Debit cards** are similar to credit cards: You use them instead of cash. The difference is that with a **debit card**, you spend your money, not the bank's. The money is **debited** or subtracted from your checking account.

   Is interest added to or **debited from** a savings account? _____

Part 2
Reading

Warm-Up Activity: Skimming

Skim the reading quickly for the information in Sentences 1–5. Mark the sentences T (true), F (false), or IE (insufficient evidence). Use IE when there is not enough information to tell if the statement is true or false. (1 or 2 minutes)

_____ 1. A commercial bank tries to expand like any other business.

_____ 2. The U.S. government sets minimum interest rates for banks.

_____ 3. In the United States, most banks compound interest daily.

_____ 4. Checks clear the bank within two weeks.

_____ 5. Debit cards came into use before credit cards.

BANKING IN THE UNITED STATES

1   Commercial banks are profit-making corporations. They compete with other banks for customers, yet this competition takes place within the rules and regulations that state and federal governments establish. For example, the U.S. federal government sets the maximum interest
5 rates on savings accounts. The government does not allow banks to pay more than this maximum rate, nor does it allow them to branch freely into other states.

      Different banks emphasize different services. Before choosing a bank, you should decide on the ones that are important to you. With
10 savings accounts, you shouldn't take it for granted that all banks pay the maximum interest rate. Be sure to ask about the interest rate. Also, it is a good idea to find out how often the bank pays interest. Most banks compound interest quarterly. When interest is compounded frequently, the customer earns more. As for checking ac-
15 counts, you should first consider the cost. Some banks offer free checking; others require a minimum balance or have a per-check charge. Next, you should find out how long it takes for a check to clear. You shouldn't assume that the time will be the same for all checks. It can vary from one or two days to several weeks. Finally,
20 you should consider the bank's location, hours, and other services. Finding a bank with every imaginable service may not be as important as finding one that is close to home, school, or workplace.

      Banks are now offering quite a few additional services, many of them due to computer technology. Credit cards and debit cards (bank-
25 cards) went into use in the 1950s and the 1980s, respectively. Drive-up windows have long been popular with people on the go. Automated teller machines were an innovation of the 1970s. A customer can use a "money machine" to check the balance in savings or checking accounts, deposit a check, withdraw cash, or make a loan payment. In

30   some places, it is also possible to bank by home computer. Banks are
      making it increasingly more convenient to use their services.

Part 3
Vocabulary Follow-Up

Subtechnical Vocabulary

A. *Check your understanding of words from the reading. As you read, think about the meaning of the words in* **boldface**.

Last month I was thinking about buying a used car. My uncle Jim told me to **consider** the purchase carefully before deciding. He told me to decide on definite **maximum** and **minimum** prices. If I didn't decide on a maximum, I might pay too much. If I didn't **set** a minimum price, I might end up with a cheap car that needed a lot of repairs.

Uncle Jim told me not to believe everything the salespeople said. I **took it for granted** that salespeople gave good advice, but Jim said to look in an authority such as *Consumer Reports* to get complete information.

"When an advertisement for a car dealership says that you can make payments of only $199 **per** month, remember that a loan from the bank sometimes costs less," Jim said. He also said that prices for the same car can **vary**. He advised me not to buy at the first dealership I went to, but to compare prices at other dealerships where the same car might be less. The salespeople I talked to **emphasized** different things. One stressed the fact that a car was cheap. Another thought it was important to have a beautiful car. Most important for me was having a dependable car.

Finally, I decided to get the Turtle, a slow but dependable car. The prices were $7550, $7100, and $7999 at Girard Motors, Sneaky Sam's Autos, and Prestige Automobile, **respectively**. At $7999, Prestige charged too much. Sneaky Sam's price of $7100 sounded good, but the service agreement for repairs was good for only two weeks. I got my Turtle at Girard Motors.

After I became a car owner, something special **took place**. I was proud of my Turtle, and I felt a new responsibility to drive carefully for my safety and the safety of people in my car. My uncle noticed what had happened and told me he liked the change.

B. *Write these words after their definitions.*

consider   set   vary   take place
maximum   take for granted   emphasize
minimum   per   respectively

1. assume, believe without evidence or proof _____

2. happen, occur _____

3. in the order given _____

4. the highest number or amount possible _____

5. the lowest number or amount possible _____

6. give stress or importance to something _____

7. for every _____

8. determine, decide on definitely, establish _____

9. think about something carefully _____

10. be different, change _____

Part 4
Understanding Through Writing

General Comprehension

Answer about the reading. When there is a choice, circle a or b.

1. In the first paragraph, the reader learns two general points about commercial banks in the United States. These two main points are that:
   a. the government sets maximum interest rates on savings accounts and doesn't allow banks to branch across state lines.
   b. banks are profit-making businesses and are regulated by the government.

2. The first paragraph gives two examples of government regulations on banks. What are these two examples?

   _____

   _____

3. The second paragraph has three parts. The first two sentences are general. There are two specific sections after that. Write the phrases that introduce these two sections.

_____   _____

4. The second paragraph gives advice. The third to the last sentence ("You shouldn't assume ....") gives advice about checks clearing. Look at the next sentence ("It can vary ...."). What is its purpose?

   a. to give advice
   b. to give more information about the previous piece of advice

5. What happens in the third paragraph?

   a. A summary of the banking advice in paragraph 2 is given.
   b. Innovations in banking services are explained.

Sentence Study: Paraphrasing

Paraphrasing is an important skill for academic work. In writing any kind of research, it is common to paraphrase other peoples' ideas. When writers paraphrase, they state someone's ideas but *not* in the same words. To paraphrase is to say the same thing using your own words.

Read this sentence:

> Commercial banks compete with other banks for customers, yet this competition takes place within the rules and regulations that state and federal governments establish.

Now read these two different paraphrases of the same idea:

Paraphrase 1: Competition among banks occurs under state and federal government laws.

Paraphrase 2: Banks compete among themselves for business but must follow regulations set by state and federal governments.

EXERCISE 1

Read the first sentence. The phrases below it are in mixed order. Use them to write a sentence that paraphrases the first sentence. A capital letter shows the beginning of each paraphrase.

   Example: The government does not allow banks to pay more than the maximum interest rate.

   can't/pay more interest/by law/Banks/than the maximum

   Banks can't pay more interest than the maximum by law.

1. Most banks compound interest quarterly.

   four times a year/pay interest/The majority of banks

   _____

2. Before choosing a bank, you should decide on the services that are important to you.

   the most helpful services/It is important/before opening an account/to determine

   _____

   _____

3. With savings accounts, you shouldn't take it for granted that all banks pay the maximum interest rate.

   can't assume/that every bank/on savings accounts/gives the best interest rate/You

   _____

   _____

4. Banks are now offering quite a few additional services, many of them due to computer technology.

   many more services/thanks to computers/currently provide/Commercial banks

   _____

   _____

Discourse Study: *One(s)/the One(s)* for Reference

One(s) refers back to indefinite nouns:

> He has a checking account at the bank on the corner from school. He also has **one** at a bank close to his home.
>
> **one** = a checking account

> I like banks with no service charges. Which **ones** have free checking?
>
> **ones** = banks

The one(s) refers back to definite nouns:

> There are several banks in the immediate area. I like **the ones** with free checking. **The one** across the street from school has automated teller cards and free checking.
>
> **the ones** = the banks
> **the one** = the bank

EXERCISE 2

See the reading to find out what these expressions refer back to. Write their meanings according to the reading.

     Examples: they, line 1 ___*commercial banks*___

                  this competition, line 2: ___*the competition between banks*___

1. *this maximum rate,* line 6: _____

2. *it,* line 6: _____

3. *them,* line 6: _____

4. *the ones,* line 9: _____

5. *others,* line 16: _____

6. *one,* line 22: _____

7. *them,* line 24: _____

8. *their services,* line 31: _____

Part 5
Getting Ready to Write Paragraphs

Conjunctions: *Yet* and *Nor*

There are seven conjunctions in English: *and, but, or, for, so, nor, yet.* Conjunctions can join two sentences. These "sentences in sentences" are called clauses:

Clause   **, BUT**   Clause

The bank manager wanted to take off early, **but** he was too busy.

All the conjunctions except *yet* and *nor* are discussed in earlier chapters. Study these rules for the more formal conjunctions *yet* and *nor.*

Yet: *Yet* shows concession; the second piece of information is unexpected:

Local banks wanted to have more money for home loans this year, **yet** their totals were far lower than last year's totals.

The tellers at these banks are slow and discourteous, **yet** they have a great many customers.

A comma comes before *yet* when joining clauses. Some writers use a semi-colon with *yet*:

> The service at this bank is painfully slow; **yet** customers continue to use it because of its convenient location.

Nor: The first clause is negative. The second clause has a comma + the negative conjunction *nor*. *Nor* means "also not":

> The bank did**n't** write to me. **Also,** they did**n't** telephone me. =
> The bank did**n't** write to me, **nor**   did   they   telephone me.

Use question word order in the clause after *nor*:

> The bank didn't write to me, nor **did they** telephone me.
> She doesn't like this bank, nor **do I**.

Giving Advice

Imperative (simple) verbs can give advice:

> **See** a loan officer right away. Please **don't delay**.

Should + a main verb also gives advice:

> You **should** open an account. = I think opening a checking account is a good idea for you.
> You **shouldn't** delay.   = I think delaying is inadvisable.

RECOGNITION EXERCISE

See the reading on page 131 to answer.

1. Find the sentence with *yet* in the first paragraph. How are the two clauses in the sentence related? (*Circle one choice.*)

   a. cause and effect
   b. concession
   c. similarity

2. Find the sentence with *nor* in the first paragraph. Rewrite the second clause as one complete sentence without *nor*. (*Change the grammar, but keep the meaning the same.*)

   _____

3. The second paragraph has sentences that give advice with *should* and imperatives. What other expression in the paragraph offers advice?

   _____

EXERCISE 3

Read the first sentence. On a separate piece of paper, combine the two sentences below it with **nor**. *Remember question word order after* **nor**.

Example: The economic situation is not good these days.

Unemployment isn't decreasing. Interest rates aren't falling.

Unemployment isn't decreasing, nor are interest rates falling.

1. We were waiting to hear about the election.
   The election results weren't available. The trends weren't clear.

2. The President was considering adding money to the space program. We wanted to hear his ideas about this when he spoke on TV.
   He didn't state a choice. He didn't discuss his ideas about it.

3. The chairman of the board told the bank president to study a particular document and to discuss it with the vice-presidents.
   The bank president didn't look at the document.
   He didn't discuss it with anyone.

4. I presented my evidence on noise pollution to a state official.
   She didn't think noise pollution was related to her work.
   She didn't think it was a large-scale problem.

5. My hometown bank doesn't have all the services that many banks do.
   My bank doesn't have free checking accounts.
   It doesn't have drive-up windows.

EXERCISE 4

Add **yet** + *a clause with unexpected information.*

Example: There are several banks in the city center, *yet none of them is close to this immediate area.*

1. This bank offers automated teller cards, _____

2. Some banks went out of business last year, _____

3. Almost all banks in the United States handle their business by computer,

4. Ordinarily, the computers allow the tellers to take care of business quickly and

   efficiently, _____

   _____

5. I like my bank, _____

   _____

EXERCISE 5

Give advice on choosing a bank, buying a used car, or another topic. Write six or more sentences with imperatives. Work on a separate piece of paper.

Example: *Ask friends for recommendations.*

Part 6
Writing Paragraphs

Warm-Up Activity

Read this recipe, and notice the verbs.

Easy Apple Pie

Wash, pare, core, and **slice** eight tart apples. **Add** ³/₄ cup sugar, 3 tablespoons flour, and 1 teaspoon cinnamon; **stir** gently. **Pour** into an unbaked pie crust (available at supermarkets). In a small bowl, **mix** ¹/₂ cup flour and ¹/₄ cup sugar. **Use** a pastry blender or fork to cut in ¹/₄ cup softened butter till crumbly. **Add** this mixture on top of the apples. **Dot** with butter. **Bake** at 400 degrees for 45 minutes or until the top browns. **Let** cool for 30 minutes before serving. **Serve** with vanilla ice cream or a slice of cheddar cheese.

Write a short paragraph in which you tell how to cook a favorite dish. Use imperative verbs to make the directions clear and direct. Give the name of the dish at the beginning. Read your recipes aloud in small groups.

Getting Started: Description of a Process

In this section, you will write a paragraph that tells how to do something. Begin by choosing a process with several steps, such as:

how to buy a new or used car	how to ask someone for a date
how to take good photographs	how to be successful in business
how to open a checking account	how to study for final exams

Write down the steps in the process; also write a general topic sentence to interest your readers. In pairs, read your topic sentences aloud. Then explain the steps in the process to your partner. Tell your partner if a step seems to be missing in his or her process.

Writing a First Draft

Begin with your topic sentence. Then concentrate on introducing the steps in the process in order. Use imperative verbs and sequence signals (*first, after that, the last step is to*, etc.). Use *one(s)/the one(s)* to refer back to nouns. Use a concluding sentence that makes a general comment about the process.

After you finish, go through your paper using the following checklist. Make changes and copy your paper over.

Checklist

1. Find a clear statement of the process that will be described.
2. Find the sequence expressions for each step. Is the order clear? If not, what changes will help to make it clearer?
3. Do you understand the process? Why or why not?
4. Is there anything that you suggest adding or removing?
5. Is it clear what *(the)one/ones* and other pronouns refer to?
6. Does the paragraph have a strong concluding statement at the end?
7. Read the paragraph one time for grammar. Then read it a second time for spelling and punctuation.

Revising the First Draft

Exchange papers with your partner for comments and suggestions. Use the checklist to go through the paper you receive. Give your partner some suggestions. Then rewrite your paragraph keeping in mind your partner's most important suggestions.

CHAPTER ELEVEN

Special Effects in the Movies

People enjoy going to the movies for different reasons. Some like to go to learn something or to become better informed. For many, movies are pure entertainment, something to do for fun and relaxation. During the last few decades, science fiction filmmakers have done a lot of work with special effects to make their movies more exciting. Special effects make it possible to show things on film that exist only in the imagination.

Part 1
Reading

Warm-Up Activity: Discussion Questions

Discuss these questions in small groups or as a class. Ask each other additional questions that come up during your discussion.

1. Do you like science fiction films? What is your favorite one? Why?

2. What popular movie today has special effects? Describe the special effects in the film. What makes them interesting or unusual?

3. How do filmmakers create special effects? How do they make it look like Superman is flying or Godzilla is destroying a building?

MOVIES WITH SPECIAL EFFECTS

1   Movies such as *King Kong* (1933), *2001: A Space Odyssey* (1968), and *Who Framed Roger Rabbit?* (1988) all have something in common: They make use of special effects to make the viewer believe the unbelievable. There is a wide range of special effects. Anything from
5   a spaceship moving across space at the speed of light to a monster destroying an entire city is possible. The success of these films depends largely on their frequent use of special effects.
    Many techniques are used to create special effects. One of these techniques is animation. Using this method, an artist paints pictures
10 on clear film. The artist creates movement by drawing the people or things in each picture in a slightly different position. Many drawings

RJB00147-29A Photo by Terry Chostner. Special effects expert Phil Tippett works with a two-legged walker from the *Star Wars* films. COURTESY OF LUCASFILM LDT.

are necessary for only a few seconds of film. Another technique is
called *matte*. Matte shots are used for large objects that cannot be
built easily, such as mountains. A painting is made on glass. It is
15 filmed and then combined with a separate film of live action. Still
another technique is the use of small models. Using close-up shots
makes models that are 4 inches high look like giant monsters, space-
ships, or space stations.

Technical innovations play a major part in the creation of realistic
20 special effects in the movies. The film printer, for example, was developed in the 1930s. This machine allows several pieces of film to be
combined into one. One piece of film might be a picture of a large
painted background; other pieces may be of models, and the last part
might be of live action with actors. All the pieces are used together for
25 a realistic effect. This machine is still in wide use today. Another innovation is the flex camera, which was developed for *Star Wars*. The
movement of the flex camera is controlled by a computer that is able
to repeat the camera movement exactly for a second filming after
changes or additions to the scene. The two machines are often used
30 together to create complex special effects.

Due to the phenomenal popularity of films with special effects,
filmmakers intend to make many more of them using the present techniques and those yet to be developed. As in years past, science fiction
movies with special effects will show movie-goers objects and beings
35 that don't exist in the real world. They will stimulate the imagination
of the public and challenge the creativity of the filmmaker.

Part 2
Vocabulary Follow-Up

Content Vocabulary: Special Effects

A. *Read for an understanding of the **boldfaced** words.*

It is interesting to watch people **film** a movie. The actors look strange because they wear a lot of makeup. There are people with cameras and sound equipment. Sometimes there is a group of people watching as well.

The **scene** for a movie is usually important. Sometimes a movie is made on location at a particular place such as the Alps or the Sahara. In other cases, the **scene** is created at a studio in Hollywood, for example.

A part of the scene for a movie is the **background**. The **background** might be mountains, a sunset over the ocean, or city skyscrapers. Often an artist will paint the **background** on glass.

One kind of **shot** is a close-up. For this, the camera is close to the actor or subject for awhile. Panning the camera is a different kind of **shot**. When the camera pans, it moves slowly to the side for a wide view.

A favorite children's activity is building a **model** from a hobby shop. After putting all the parts of the **model** together, the child has a tiny three-dimensional representation of a submarine, car, plane, etc. A **model** is sometimes more fun than the actual full-sized object.

We saw a science fiction movie last week. The main character was a **being** with a hairy body and two heads. It ate human **beings**.

A werewolf is a kind of **monster**. This **monster** is a normal person most of the time, but when there is a full moon, the person becomes a wolf with human intelligence. The wolf bites people; then they become werewolves.

The Russians and the Americans have played the major roles in **space** travel since the early 1960s. The first person on a trip around the world in **space** was Yuri Gagarin of the U.S.S.R.

A **spaceship** called Vostok 1 took Gagarin on his trip through space. He went around the world one time in just over 89 minutes.

Solyut and Skylab were the first Russian and American **space stations** that traveled around the earth. The people who lived on these **space stations** proved that humans can live in space for at least three months.

B. *Check your understanding. Fill in the blanks with these words.*

background	model	shot	space station
being	monster	space	
film (*v*)	✔ scene	spaceship	

Example: The ____scene____ is the place where the action of a movie happens.

1. A _____ is a part of the scene for a movie. It is the part at the back, behind the actors.

2. When someone wants to _____ something, the person wants to take a moving picture of it, to put it on film.

3. _____ is the unlimited area outside the earth's atmosphere.

4. A _____ is a sequence of action that is photo-graphed by a movie camera.

5. A _____ is an artificial satellite that people can live on and that travels around the earth.

6. A _____ is a small copy of a large object.

7. A _____ is any type of living animal.

8. A _____ is a huge, ugly, imaginary animal that is unnatural and frightening.

9. A _____ is a vehicle used to carry people and things from earth to the moon, to the planets, or to a space station.

Part 3
Understanding Through Writing

General Comprehension: Inferences

An inference is an educated guess or conclusion that you can make from the facts given. Read these facts:

Mickey Mouse was one of the first big stars of animation. He was created by cartoonist Walt Disney in 1928. For decades, Mickey and his girlfriend Minnie have delighted movie-going audiences. Old Mickey and Minnie cartoons are available today on video and can be rented inexpensively at video stores.

Based on this information, is the following inference logical?

Mickey Mouse has been popular with several generations of children.

You know that Mickey was created in 1928 and that people have enjoyed him "for decades." Thinking about the period of time between 1928 and now, "several generations" of children have grown up. (Father, son, and grandson are three generations.) Mickey's popularity is clear because the information says that he was a "big star." It is therefore safe to say that he has been "popular with several generations of children."

Now think about this statement:

Mickey Mouse is the most popular animated cartoon character.

This is not a logical inference. The information says that Mickey was "one of the first big stars" and that he has been very popular. It is not clear that he is "the most popular cartoon character." (It might be true, but it is not a good inference from the information given.)

*Based on the information in the reading, decide if these are logical or illogical inferences. Mark each **logical** or **illogical**.*

1. _____ Using special effects techniques, film producers can create almost any imaginable scene.
2. _____ The film printer will continue to be used for special effects films for years to come.
3. _____ No new techniques will be developed for special effects movies since there is a wide variety already available.
4. _____ When space travel teaches us more about the other planets in our solar system, interest in science fiction films will decrease.

Discuss your answers in small groups. Use sentences from the reading to explain your choices.

Word Study

Write words from the reading.

	Location	Meaning	Word or Expression
1.	line 2	share	*have in common*
2.	line 3	use (verb)	_____

Location	Meaning	Word or Expression
3. line 4	all possible variations, scope	_____
4. line 7	is determined by	_____
5. line 16	a way of doing something	_____
6. line 17	huge, very large	_____
7. line 25	used a lot	_____
8. line 27	can	_____
9. line 34	people who go to movies	_____
10. line 35	cause increased activity	_____
11. line 36	people	_____

Sentence Study: Paraphrasing

Paraphrasing means stating an idea using your own words. Read this idea:

Movies such as *King Kong* (1933), *2001: A Space Odyssey* (1968), and *Who Framed Roger Rabbit?* (1988) all have something in common: They make use of special effects to make the viewer believe the unbelievable.

Now read two paraphrases of that same idea:

Science fiction films use special effects to make viewers believe that something unreal is real.

In science fiction films, things that seem impossible are made to look real because of special effects.

Which expression in the original statement is repeated in the paraphrases? Why is it repeated exactly? (Why doesn't the writer paraphrase this expression?)

Read the first sentence. Then cover it up as you complete the second sentence in a way that gives it the same meaning. Use your own words. After you finish, compare and discuss sentences with a partner.

Example: Technical innovations play a major part in the creation of realistic special effects in the movies.

Making special effects that look real *is largely the result of new technology in filmmaking.*

1. Many techniques are used to create special effects.

Special effects are achieved through the use of _____

_____

2. The success of science fiction films depends largely on their frequent use of special effects.

The use of many special effects _____

_____

3. Due to the phenomenal popularity of films with special effects, film-makers intend to make many more of them.

Filmmakers will continue to make movies with special effects because

_____

Discourse Study: Using Synonyms

In English, writers will often use a synonym instead of using the same word over and over:

Science fiction movies make good use of special effects. **These films** use more special effects than other types of films.

These films refers to "science fiction movies." The use of *these* also helps the reader to understand that "films" refers back to the "science fiction movies" mentioned earlier.

Find each word in the reading. Then continue reading until you find a synonym. Write the synonyms in the blanks.

Example: line 1, *movies such as "King Kong"* = ___*these films*___

1. line 8, *techniques* = _____

2. line 11, *picture* = _____

3. line 20, *the film printer* = _____

4. line 22, *piece* = ____ _____

Part 4
Getting Ready to Write Paragraphs

The Colon (:)

The colon is used in two different ways.

1. To introduce a list of things:

At the beginning of the film, Jack tells Sandra that she has three choices for her birthday: a short trip to see his mother, a longer trip to see his brother, or a week-long trip to the Caribbean.

2. To introduce a specific explanation or example of a general statement:

> After several scenes from their last trip, the action returns to the couple, and Sandra tells Jack some bad news**:** **T**hey don't actually have enough money for any trip at all.

Note the capital letter after a colon when it is followed by a sentence.

Subject Signals with *Other*

Forms of *other* are often used as subject signals in a paragraph. They point out when a new reason, example, cause, result, etc., begins. The form is *(an)other* + adjective + noun:

> **One problem** is that they lack money for a trip. There is less than $100 in their savings account. **Another major difficulty** is that they don't have nearly enough time. **Still another problem** is their pet dog.

Writing Conclusions

One way to conclude writing is to restate the main points. Another possibility is to make a prediction for the future. *Will* is more formal than *be going to*, so *will* is used in writing a predictive conclusion. Either of these sentences could finalize the ideas about Jack and Sandra:

> They **will** probably **wait** until next year for a trip to the Caribbean.
> (OR)
> Jack and Sandra **will not be able to take** a trip this year.

Verbs with Future Meaning

The verbs in these examples show future time without *will* or *be going to*:

> They **want to** go to the Caribbean.
> They **intend to** go next year.
> The woman **promises to** save money.
> She **needs to** make fewer purchases.
> They **expect to** live cheaply this year.
> They **plan to** take the trip next year.

RECOGNITION EXERCISE

See the reading on page 141 to answer.

1. A colon is used after the expression *have something in common* in paragraph 1. Does the colon introduce a list of items or explain the previous statement?

   _____

2. The first subject signal in paragraph 2 is *one of these techniques.* What are the other two subject signals?

   _____   _____

3. Write the two sentences in paragraph 3 that introduce examples.

   _____

   _____

4. What kind of concluding paragraph is used in the reading? Does the conclusion re-state main points or make predictions?

   _____

EXERCISE 1

Answer in complete sentences on a separate piece of paper.

   Example: What do you plan to do tonight?

   I plan to see a film on campus tonight.

1. What do you plan to do tonight?
2. What do you promise to do soon?
3. What do you intend to do next year?
4. Where do you expect to live next year?
5. What do you need to do this week?
6. Where do you want to go this summer?

EXERCISE 2

Explain or give examples after the colons in these sentences. Copy and complete the sentences on another piece of paper.

   Examples: I'm taking two classes: *art history and biology.*

   I don't like the biology class: *There are too many details to learn.*

1. I have several friends from other countries:

2. We enjoy lots of activities together:

3. My friends help me not to feel homesick:

4. We all saw a couple of films together recently:

5. I enjoy spending time with my friends:

6. There is one principal reason that I don't like _____ :

   (*Fill in the blank with something that you don't like.*)

7. There are several advantages to _____ :

   (*Fill in the blank with something to which there are advantages.*)

EXERCISE 3

Read the paragraphs. Add periods and colons where needed. Write subject signals with **other** *+ adjective + noun in the blanks. Also complete the predictive conclusion.*

Science fiction films, especially space fantasies, have long been popular with movie-going audiences   It is the special effects in these films that makes for their success   Filmmakers of today have been schooled in the use of special effects techniques by films from the beginning of the 20th century   *A Trip to the Moon* (1902), *King Kong* (1933), and *Things to Come* (1936).

Georges Melie had previous work experience that served him well when he became the first special effects filmmaker   He had been a magician for years   His special effects in *A Trip to the Moon* created the first space fantasy and the first international success   _____

is Peter Ellenshaw, who worked 26 years in the Walt Disney studios   His effects during the dance of the chimney sweeps on London rooftops in *Mary Poppins* proved that special effects worked well with color film   _____

is John Dykstra, who supervised the effects for milestone movies from the more recent past   *Star Wars* and *Star Trek*, among others   As we approach a new century, young effects technicians and artists such as Dykstra will _____

Part 5
Writing Paragraphs

Warm-Up Activity: Writing Conclusions

Write a different paragraph of conclusion for the reading on page 141. One choice is to write a predictive conclusion using *will*. Another possibility is to write a conclusion that summarizes the main points of the reading.

To do this, paraphrase the main ideas (as expressed by the topic sentences) of each paragraph. Compare completed paragraphs with one or two students.

Getting Started: Paragraphs of Prediction

Choose a topic from the following suggestions. Make a list of details that you may want to include in your discussion. Then read over your details and make sure that they all relate directly to your topic. Write a topic sentence for your paragraph. Show your list and topic sentence to a partner for discussion. Make additions and changes after your discussion. Remove any details that aren't closely related to your topic.

1. Write a paragraph that tells what will probably happen in your life in the future. Use *will* and verbs like *intend to*, *need to*, *want to*, etc. Use subject signals with *other* to introduce points in the paragraph. Begin with a general topic sentence about your future.
2. Predict a future world event. Tell what will probably happen and why. Make the paragraph a realistic or an imaginary view of the future.
3. Palmistry is a tool of folk psychology. Study the palm diagram. This diagram shows the location of some of the lines and other areas that palm readers use to predict someone's future. Read the information about each area of the hand. Work with a partner who has chosen this topic also. Read each other's palms. Make up an imaginary story about the person's future. If you prefer to work alone, read your own palm.

Physical Characteristic	*Character Trait*
long, clear head line	a lot of interests
long head, heart, or life lines	strong character
heart line forms a fork at the end	warm-hearted, emotional
many lines	intellectual
few lines	skilled with hands
head and life lines joined	clear speaker
small hands	like big projects
big hands	analytical
big hands and long fingers	very analytical
strong, wide hands	practical, full of energy
narrow hands	nervous, introspective
graceful hands	inner balance

If any area of the palm is large or noticeable, these characteristics are emphasized:

```
Venus   = warmth, vitality, love of luxury and the senses
Moon    = imaginative, restless
Mercury = observant, good speaker
Apollo  = artistic, good sense of style
Saturn  = serious, down to earth
Jupiter = ambitious, a leader
```

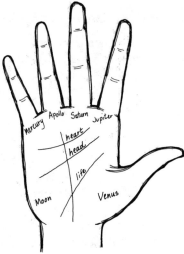

Writing a First Draft

Begin with your topic sentence; then discuss the details on your list. For now, think only about getting your ideas down. Remember these points:

1. The topic sentence limits the discussion in a paragraph.
2. The topic sentence is supported by specific detail.
3. The specific details all relate to the central idea of the paragraph as expressed by the topic sentence.

After you finish, read your paragraph. Find one or two places to use synonyms instead of repeating nouns. Use the following checklist to go over your paper. Make changes, and copy the paragraph for your partner to read.

Checklist

1. Find a clear statement of the topic of the paragraph.
2. Find sentences with specific discussion of the main idea of the paragraph. Do all the sentences relate to the main idea?
3. Do you suggest adding or removing any material?
4. Find one or two places where the writer uses synonyms effectively.
5. Read the paragraph one time to check all the future verbs. Then read it a second time for spelling and punctuation.
6. What is the best part of the paragraph? Why?

Revising the First Draft

Exchange papers with your partner for suggestions and discussion. Use the checklist to go through the paper. Underline and ask about anything that is not clear to you.

Help your partner to improve the style of the paragraph: If there are a lot of short sentences, combine some of them using *and, but, so, nor, because,* a semicolon, etc. If there are sentences that are difficult to understand because they are so long, work with your partner and divide them into shorter, clearer sentences.

Rewrite your paper based on your partner's most important suggestions.

CHAPTER TWELVE

Standardized Tests

College students in the United States take many tests. There are special tests to gain entrance to colleges and universities as well. The Scholastic Aptitude Test (SAT) and the Graduate Record Examination (GRE) are examples of entrance exams. The Test of English as a Foreign Language (TOEFL) is required of students whose first language is not English. These standardized tests are designed and scored by the Educational Testing Service.

Part 1
Vocabulary in Context

Content Vocabulary: Standardized Tests

Read these paragraphs for an understanding of the words in boldface.

> The Test of English as a Foreign Language (TOEFL) is used by many colleges and universities in the United States and in other English-speaking countries to determine **eligibility** for entrance. The test measures the English language ability of non-native speakers of English. Many schools require a **score** of 500 to 550 on the TOEFL before a student can be admitted. The **administration** of this test takes about 3 hours. Students who want to improve their scores can take it again.
> The TOEFL is a multiple-choice exam. In many countries, answers on tests are typically written, but the questions on the TOEFL are multiple choice. The student selects one answer from three or four possibilities and marks it on an **answer sheet**. The **skill areas** on the TOEFL are listening comprehension, structure and written expression, and vocabulary and reading comprehension. The Educational Testing Service (ETS) also has separate tests of spoken and written English, which some schools require.

Students should ask at their language school for a **Bulletin of Information** that describes the procedure of applying for and taking the TOEFL. If a *Bulletin* is not available, students can obtain one by writing to the Educational Testing Service, Princeton, NJ 08541 USA. They should be sure to indicate the country in which they wish to take the test. In addition to reading the *Bulletin*, students can **prepare for** the TOEFL in many ways. ETS offers Test Kits, Sample Tests, and other study aids. Commercial **study guides** also provide information on test taking as well as practice tests. Heinle and Heinle, Cliffs Notes, and Barron's, among others, produce **study guides**.

Write the letter of each word next to its definition.

a. administration	e. prepare for
✓ b. answer sheet	f. score
c. *Bulletin of Information*	g. skill areas
d. eligibility	h. study guide

Example: __b__ the paper used to mark answers on a standardized test

1. _____ the different abilities tested by a standardized test

2. _____ a booklet published by ETS to indicate general procedures

3. _____ the giving of a test

4. _____ get ready for something in advance

5. _____ performance on a test, often expressed as a number or percentage

6. _____ a type of book that helps students to prepare for standardized tests

7. _____ qualification for admission to a college or university

Part 2
Reading

Warm-Up Activity: Finding the Main Idea

In pairs, read the essay on standardized tests quickly, one paragraph at a time. Decide together on the main idea (as expressed by a topic sentence) of each paragraph. Discuss your answers in small groups and/or as a class.

TAKING STANDARDIZED TESTS

1   Most students must take one or more standardized tests to enter a college or university in the United States. Because these tests are commonly used to help determine entrance eligibility, students should learn about the factors that affect scores on standardized tests. They should become familiar with the kinds of questions and answers on the tests they will take. It is also important to be aware of the skill areas on standardized tests. Students should know that the TOEFL, the SAT, the GRE, the GMAT, and other tests emphasize different skills.

2   Standardized tests are similar to one another in many ways. To begin with, they are all timed tests that are given to large groups of people. Secondly, they are multiple-choice exams scored by computer. Another similarity among standardized tests is that they require strong reading and vocabulary skills on the part of the test taker. Still another similarity is that "many kinds of tasks are likely to be encountered: making judgments, drawing conclusions, identifying what has been implied, summarizing and making generalizations, determining meanings through context, identifying what was *not* stated or implied, and so on."[1]

3   There are differences among tests as well. One factor to consider before you take a standardized test is penalty for guessing, which differs from test to test. At this writing, the TOEFL and the ACT do not penalize for guessing, but the SAT, GMAT, and GRE do. What this means is that if you guess some answers on the latter tests, you may lower your score. Let's say that on the first six questions of the SAT, a student knows the answer to two of the questions but guesses incorrectly on the other four. When there are errors, the computer will subtract points. Often the penalty is minus one-fourth point for each wrong guess. The student in our example, then, receives only one point for the two correct answers because there were also four incorrect answers.

4   You can best prepare for a standardized test by starting well in advance. To make sure that you will be able to take the test on the date and at the testing center of your choice, you should apply for the test early. It is also a good idea to get a *Bulletin of Information* for the particular test you will be taking. The *Bulletin* will answer many questions about the test. Using a study guide is another way to prepare. Study guides provide both general and specific information and include practice tests. You can analyze your abilities by taking the practice tests; further preparation should focus on the weakest skill area for the greatest gain. In short, there are many things you can do to improve your score on a standardized test.

5   Reading the test directions seems simple, but it is more important than many people realize. A final piece of advice is this: "During the test administration, read all the test directions carefully. Since many completed answer sheets indicate that examinees do not follow directions, this suggestion is particularly important."[2]

Part 3
Vocabulary Follow-Up

Subtechnical Vocabulary: Synonyms

Check your understanding of words from the reading. Under-
line a synonym for each word in **boldface***. The synonym may*
be a word or a phrase.

Example: In writing a long paper, the first job is to **determine** a good, specific topic. This is easier said than done. After general reading on the topic, the writer can <u>decide on</u> a specific topic.

1. It is **likely** that this first step, determining a topic, will be one of the hardest things to do in writing the paper. The writer must read a lot before deciding on a specific topic for a long paper. It is probable that other steps will also be challenging.

2. For example, **making a judgment** about what to include and what not to include is sometimes difficult. It takes time to consider the facts and form an opinion.
3. It often works well to **focus** the discussion of a paper on only a few major points. This way, both writer and reader can direct attention to the important parts of the paper.
4. The writer often expresses the main points of the paper as **generalizations**. Giving a general statement and then discussing it more specifically is a common way to organize writing in English.
5. Another method of organization for writing a paper is chronological (time) order. We **encounter** this kind of organization when the topic is historical, for example. We also find chronological organization when a sequence of actions or events is important.
6. Writing styles **differ** from language to language. In English, it is important to write in a way that is direct and brief. English writing style is different in this respect from Arabic, Japanese, Spanish, and French, for example.
7. When people write in a way that is direct, they don't suggest ideas; they state them. Many writers in English think that direct expression

is important. Good writers also **imply** ideas, but in academic writing, ideas are stated directly for the most part.

8. After writing a paper in rough form, the writer must **analyze** the paper carefully. After looking critically at the paper, the writer makes changes to improve organization and expression.

Part 4
Understanding Through Writing

General Comprehension: Implication and Direct Statement

When writers imply an idea, they suggest it but don't state it directly. *Based on information in the reading, mark these statements I (implied), S (stated), or N (neither implied nor stated).*

Examples: __I__ Good readers do well on standardized tests.

__S__ Standardized tests are used by U.S. colleges and universities to decide on applicants.

__N__ Students who use study guides can expect to get scores that are twice as high as students who don't.

____ 1. Standardized tests are timed tests.

____ 2. It is best to prepare in the weakest skill area because it is easier to improve a lot in a weak area than it is to improve a lot in an area that is already strong.

____ 3. You cannot take a standardized test by yourself.

____ 4. If you are taking the TOEFL, you should guess answers you don't know.

____ 5. There are certain basic skills required of all standardized tests.

____ 6. The more expensive study guides are the best for students.

Go over your answers in pairs or small groups. Use sentences from the reading to show why your answers are correct.

Sentence Study: Paraphrasing

Read these sentences. Then complete the paraphrases for each. Cover the first sentence and state the same idea using your own words. When you finish, compare paraphrases with a partner.

Example: Most students must take one or more standardized tests to enter a college or university in the United States.

Students typically take at least one standardized test to _qualify for higher education in the United States._

1. Students should know that the TOEFL, the SAT, the GRE, the GMAT, and other tests emphasize different skill areas.

   It is important for students to understand that _____

   _____

2. Standardized tests are similar to one another in many ways.

   There are quite a few similarities _____

3. When there are errors, the computer will subtract points.

   The computer lowers a score for _____

4. You can best prepare for a standardized test by starting well in advance.

   To maximize your chances for a good score, you _____

   _____

Discourse Study: Organizing a Longer Piece of Writing

Number these topics in the order they are discussed (by paragraph) in the reading.

_____ similarities between

_____ how to prepare for

_____ the importance of reading the directions

__1__ general information about standardized tests

_____ differences among

A list of main points like this helps writers to organize their writing. For longer papers, an outline is used. An outline shows the relationships between major and supporting ideas. Each paragraph (or section) of the paper is a major category in the outline and has a Roman numeral (I, II, etc.). Main points for each paragraph have capital letters. Further detail is given with Arabic numbers.

See the reading on page 156. Fill in the missing topics and subtopics of paragraphs in this outline of the reading.

I. General Information about Standardized Tests
   A. Necessary for most students
   B. Importance of learning about factors that affect scores

      1. kinds of questions and answers

      2. _skill area emphasis_ _____

II. Similarities among Standardized Tests
    A. Timed exams for large groups

    B. _____

    C. Require strong reading and vocabulary
    D. Thinking skills/tasks on standardized tests

       1. _____

       2. _____

       3. identifying what has been implied

       4. _____

       5. determining meanings through context

       6. _____

III. _____

     A. Penalty for guessing differs from test to test
     B. Explanatory example of penalty for guessing

IV. How to Prepare for a Standardized Test
    A. Start early

    B. _____

    C. Get a *Bulletin of Information*

    D. _____

V. _____

Part 5
Getting Ready to Write a Composition

Decide which sentences are generalizations (general statements) and which give specifics. Mark them G (general) or S (specific).

1. _____ Almost all standardized tests have a multiple-choice format.

2. _____ The GRE is an example of a standardized test.

3. _____ In summary, we are open to many possibilities.

4. _____ For instance, fish are *poikilothermous*, or cold-blooded.

5. _____ Secondly, the reports were poorly typed.

6. _____ There are people for whom practice of those techniques is helpful.

7. _____ Another problem is that people don't care much about this election.

Making General Statements

You have worked with many ways to make general statements in earlier chapters. Review the forms that make a general statement.

Expressions of Quantity	Adverbs of Frequency	Adjectives and *-ly* Adverbs
most	almost always	common/commonly
many/much	usually	ordinary/ordinarily
the majority	often	usual/usually
almost all	seldom	typical/typically

Most students are a little bit nervous when they're taking tests. Students **ordinarily** feel nervous before taking a standardized test. Advisors **usually** suggest getting a good night's sleep before the exam.

Present Tense and *There + Be*

Students **do** a better job on tests when they are mentally alert. **There are** benefits when students **eat** and **sleep** well before taking a test.

Plural Nouns, Indefinite Noun Phrases

Standardized tests (= all standardized tests) take a long time. Students have a lot of nervous energy when taking **a standardized test** (= any standardized test).

Expressions of Generalization

generally	as a rule
generally speaking	for the most part
in general	on the whole

As a rule, students feel well-prepared by the test date when they work for two to four months with study guides.

Summary Statements

to summarize	in short
in summary	simply stated
to sum up	in conclusion
to review the facts	briefly then

Simply stated, test scores may improve considerably when students prepare carefully.

Introducing Specifics

When introducing examples, writers give variety to their style by combining different expressions, for example, *to begin with*, *secondly*, and *a final result* instead of *first*, *second*, *third*. Review forms to introduce specific examples.

Expressions for Introducing Examples

for example	for one thing
for instance	to illustrate
to give an example	to give a specific instance

For example, if you don't eat before taking the TOEFL, you will probably get hungry before the test is over.

For one thing, not eating before taking the TOEFL will result in being hungry before the test is over.

Sequence Expressions

Sequence expressions can indicate chronological (time) order for:

1. the events in a narrative
2. the steps in a process

first, first of all, to begin with
second, secondly
then, next, after that, afterward, later, subsequently
finally, in the end

First, first of all, second(ly), and *finally* can also introduce reasons, similarities, causes, or other examples:

It is wise to pay particular attention to your health when you have to take a standardized test. **First of all**, you should be sure to eat some protein on the morning of the test.

Subject Signals

one result	a first cause
another result	a second cause
still another effect	an additional factor

One result is that you will have plenty of mental energy.
Another result is that you will be able to work for a long time.

RECOGNITION EXERCISE

See the reading on page 156 to answer.

1. What makes paragraph 1 of the reading general? Look at the paragraph and pick out the words and expressions which indicate that the paragraph is general. Write three of them.

    _____ _____ _____

2. What makes the first sentence of paragraph 2 general? Write two key words or expressions.

    _____ _____

3. The examples in paragraph 2 are signaled in different ways. How are they signaled to the reader? Write the four expressions.

    _____ _____

    _____ _____

4. How is the topic sentence in paragraph 3 supported? (*Circle one choice.*)

    a. by the use of one lengthy example
    b. by explaining the many differences
    c. by giving several examples

5. What word in paragraph 5 shows that the writer is finishing? _____

Part 6
Writing a Composition

Warm-Up Activity: Using Direct Quotations

When you quote someone directly, you use their exact words in your writing. Quotations, especially those from well-known authorities, help to support your ideas. Writers indicate short quotations by using a comma and then quotation marks (") at the beginning and end of the material:

> According to the *GMAT Bulletin*, "Scores will not be canceled at your request for any reason once they have been reported."

When writers quote an authority, they must tell the readers where the information comes from. The source is often an article or book; sometimes it is a speech or personal communication. A number typed one-half space above the line shows that the reader can find the source of the information in the references section at the end of the paper. The information is called a *footnote* or *endnote*.

Find the two quotations in the reading for this chapter. Which of the two is more interesting to you? For which one do you want to know the source?

Write the title and author, if any, of the source for either endnote 1 or 2. See "References" on page 168 to get the information.

Getting Started

In this section, you will write a longer paper of three to five paragraphs. To begin, review this material:

A longer paper has an introductory paragraph to indicate the topic, explain which aspect of the topic will be discussed (limit the topic), and/or tell the writer's point of view about the topic (thesis statement). Sometimes the introductory paragraph gets the reader's attention by saying something interesting or surprising about the topic. The introductory paragraph of a composition has the same function as the topic sentence in a paragraph.

The second section of a composition is the discussion. This section can be from one to many paragraphs in length. A common way to organize the discussion is to decide on the number of main points to use in support of the introductory paragraph and to write one paragraph for each main point. The main points of the paragraphs in the discussion section must be supported by the content of those paragraphs. The discussion section of a composition is similar to the discussion in a paragraph, except that in a composition, each main point is supported in more detail.

The last section of a composition is one or more paragraphs of conclusion. The purpose is the same as the purpose of a concluding statement in a paragraph: to summarize the main points, to emphasize the central idea or thesis, to draw a conclusion, to make a prediction for the future, to extend the topic to something related, and so on.

Which purpose describes the last paragraph of the reading in this chapter?

Choosing a Topic

Choose a topic from the following list, or think of something different that is more interesting to you. Begin by thinking about the topic. Brainstorm for a while by just writing down any words and ideas that come to mind for the topic you choose. Then explore the topic with a partner. Discuss both your topic and your partner's topic. Write down any new vocabulary you learn or words that are common to your topic.

Topic Suggestions:

1. how to prepare for a standardized test
2. how to prepare for an exam in your field of study
3. how to manage time efficiently
4. the beneficial results of staying fit

5. the importance/benefits/recent discovery of a natural resource or agricultural product in (*country*)
6. human qualities that are beneficial in a world leader
7. an energy source of the future

Getting Organized

1. Decide on a central idea for the composition. This will allow you to make decisions about how to limit the discussion.
2. Write down the main points you want to discuss in the paper. Use an outline or a simple list. Each main point will be a paragraph.
3. Paragraphs of the composition will be organized differently. One paragraph may be general explanation, a second may give reasons, and a third might use a long narrative example. Think about how to organize the support in your paragraphs (explanation with examples, narration, description, description of a process, classification, argumentation, cause and effect, prediction). Decide on supporting material to develop each paragraph. Include a quotation where appropriate.
4. Write a statement of the central idea for the first paragraph. Then rewrite each main point as the topic sentence of a paragraph. See "Making General Statements" on page 161 for ideas.

Agriculture in Thailand

Main Points:
- *general information*
  about 70% of land used in agri.
  about ¾ of workers live in the
  fertile central plain
- *principal products*
  rice, rubber, corn, tapioca,
  sugar, pineapples
- *exports*
  rice, tapioca, sugar
  to Japan, U.S. Singapore, West
  Germany, Netherlands, U.K.
- *future plans for agri. development*

Main Points Rewritten as Topic Sentences:
In Thailand agriculture has an important role in the economy of the country.

There are many agricultural products grown in Thailand.

Thailand exports many of its agricultural products to other countries.

The government of Thailand plans to increase agricultural production in the future.

5. Copy over your notes including main points and topic sentences. Exchange papers with a partner. Give your partner any help you can. Look for one paragraph that needs more support of the main idea. Suggest additional ideas.

Writing the First Draft

Use your notes to structure your writing. Work through the outline paragraph by paragraph. Write an introductory paragraph stating the central idea of the paper, limiting the topic, showing the importance of the topic, etc. Write a separate paragraph for each main point. Support the topic sentence for each paragraph with more specific examples, reasons, results, causes, factors, advantages, things to consider, ways of doing something, etc. Write a final paragraph that summarizes the main points, emphasizes the central idea, makes a conclusion or a prediction, etc.

After you finish, read your paper critically. Have you stated your ideas clearly? Use the following checklist to go over your paper. Make the changes you want to, and copy the composition for your partner to read.

Checklist

1. Read the entire composition. What is it about? Write a title for it.
2. What makes the introductory paragraph interesting? What else might be interesting to include?
3. Find a clearly stated topic sentence/thesis statement for each paragraph. Are these statements well supported? What examples, explanation, or other detail do you suggest adding?
4. Review the main idea of each paragraph. Do they all relate to the central idea or topic of the composition? What, if anything, do you suggest removing?
5. Find places where examples are given. Are they introduced clearly? Is there a variety in the style? (Refer to "Introducing Specifics" on page 162 for ideas on how to give variety to introducing specific points.)
6. Reread the concluding paragraph. Has the writer made a prediction or conclusion, reviewed the main points, reemphasized the central idea, or extended the topic? Make one suggestion for a strong concluding paragraph.
7. Read the paper one time for grammar. Then read it a second time for spelling and punctuation.

Revising the First Draft

Trade papers with your partner, and analyze the paper you receive. Use the checklist to go over the composition. Underline and then ask about anything that is unclear. Discuss your papers together. Revise your composition according to your partner's analysis and suggestions.

References and End Notes

These references provided factual information for the readings.

Chapter One

Statistical Abstract of the United States, 101st ed. (Washington, D.C.: U.S. Bureau of the Census, 1980), p. 145.

Chapter Two

"Telephone," *Encyclopedia Britannica* (1972), *21*, 779–80.

Chapter Three

David J. Rackman, *Retailing Strategy and Structure: A Management Approach* (Englewood Cliffs, NJ: Prentice-Hall, Inc., 1969), p. 3.

Chapter Eight

Stuart G. Tipton, "Airline Challenges for the Future," *Datamation*, March 1969, p. 22.

George A. Buchanan, "The Outlook for Improved Passenger Systems," *Datamation*, March 1969, p. 25.

Chapter Nine

"Fast-Food Chains," *Consumer Reports*, September 1979, p. 508.

Dan Cook, "The Fast-Food Industry Is Slowing Down," *Business Week*, May 18, 1987, pp. 50–51.

Christopher Garrity, Assistant, Customer Relations, McDonald's Corporation, personal communication.

"McDonald's and the New American Landscape," *USA Today*, January 1980, p. 47.

Joseph Monninger, "Fast Food," *American Heritage*, April 1988, pp. 68–75.

Penny Moser, "The McDonald's Mystique," *Fortune*, July 4, 1988, pp. 112–116.

Susan E. Shank, "Women and the Labor Market: the Link Grows Stronger," *Monthly Labor Review*, U.S. Dept. of Labor, Bureau of Labor Statistics, March 1988, pp. 3–8.

Chapter Twelve

Charles Oliver, *How to Take Standardized Tests* (Englewood Cliffs, NJ: Prentice-Hall, Inc., 1981), p. 2.

GMAT 1987-88 Bulletin of Information (Princeton, NJ: Graduate Management Admission Council, Educational Testing Service, 1987), p. 12.

Answer Key

This key has answers for these sections: "Vocabulary in Context," "Reading," "Understanding Through Writing," and "Getting Ready to Write." There will be variation in wording on sentence and paraphrasing exercises. This answer key gives only some possibilities.

Chapter One

Part 1   Vocabulary in Context

Content Vocabulary

1. algebra, geometry, trigonometry, calculus, etc.
2. a. Yes, it is.
   b. No, it isn't.
3. Jack—undergraduate; Janet—graduate.
4. a. a B.A. (or bachelor's degree)
   b. a Ph.D. (or doctorate)
5. Answers will vary.
6. _A_ English literature   _A_ Architecture   _V_ TV repair

   _V_ Food service   _V_ Carpentry   _A_ Art history

   _A_ Chemistry   _V_ Secretarial skills   _A_ Biology

Subtechnical Vocabulary

1. b   3. a   5. b   7. b
2. b   4. b   6. a

Part 3   Understanding Through Writing

General Comprehension

Answers will vary in the examples of degrees. See page 169.

Part 4   Getting Ready to Write Paragraphs

Exercise 1

Today I'm going to talk about how to choose a college or university. There are many schools in this country. It's hard to decide which ones are best for you. I had the same problem 20 years ago.

The first thing to think about is getting information about schools. Your college library has a lot of college catalogs. They give important information about each school: programs, courses, applications, and housing. Look at several catalogs for the area you're interested in. I wanted to be in southern California, so I applied to UCLA, UCSD, USC, and the University of Redlands. Look first at the schools in your favorite city. You will have a good idea of the programs at the schools after you read some catalogs.

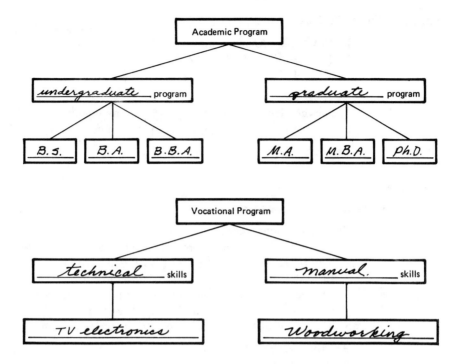

Another way to get information about schools is to talk to an advisor and to students in your major field of study. It's a good idea to visit the schools, see the campuses, talk to an advisor, and then decide.

Exercise 2 Answers will vary slightly:
1. **Academic and vocational programs are** two post-secondary programs.
2. **The B.S., the B.A., and the B.Ed. are** three examples of undergraduate degrees.
3. Three examples of graduate degrees **are the M.A., the M.S., and the M.B.A.**
4. **TV electronics and woodworking are** two examples of vocational skills.

Exercise 3 Answers will vary.

There are several types of technical education in Newcountry. Students can study engineering, computer science, and telecommunications. These are the fields of study that Newcountry and its economy need most. Students can study many types of engineering. The country needs transportation and electronics engineers. In the area of computer science, students can study software production and applications of computers in business. Telecommunications is very important in business and government. It is a career for the present and future. The young people of Newcountry are working hard to prepare themselves for many careers of the future.

Part 5   Using Prefixes

Exercise 4   Answers may vary.
1. T   3. F   5. F   7. F
2. T   4. T   6. F

Exercise 5
1. nonvocational   3. correct   5. unintelligent   7. healthy
2. interesting   4. expensive 6. common   8. possible

Exercise 6   Answers will vary.

Chapter Two

Part 1   Vocabulary in Context

Content Vocabulary

1. Today his idea is an improvement on the bicycle.   idea: *a*
2. The bicycle is slow. It is hard work going uphill.   improvement: *d*
3. In Roderic's mind is a picture of a better bicycle.   imagine: *f*
4. The equipment is simple: an electric battery and a small machine to make the wheels go around.   equipment: c
5. The result of his work is an electric bicycle.   result: *b*

Subtechnical Vocabulary

A. 1. work with
   2. three inventors all working on one problem
   3. don't stop; tell us more
B. 1. a. Answers will vary.
      b. Answers will vary.
      c. Yes, it is.
   2. Answers will vary.
   3. a. the number of miles
      b. Answers will vary.
   4. a. nine calls but no more
      b. Answers will vary.

Part 3   Understanding Through Writing

Word Study

1. unthinkable   2. over the years   3. at present   4. thanks to

Sentence Study

1. The inventors were from Germany, Italy, France, England, Denmark, Sweden, and the United States.
2. The two Englishmen were C.A. McEvoy and G.E. Pritchett.
3. Krarup was an inventor.
4. The three instruments of communication are computers, satellites, and telecopiers.

Discourse Study

1. a. international communication

b. in seconds

c. yes

2. b and c

3. b

4. b

Part 4   Getting Ready to Write Paragraphs

Recognition Exercise

1. different
2. two problems
3. a. a difference

   b. Answers will vary: I have a telephone, **but it's not working now.**
4. a. two

   b. and
5. The telephone was for local calls only because the sound traveled only a few miles.

Exercise 1

1. The Model T was much faster than horses, and it was fun and exciting.
2. The ballpoint pen makes writing easy, and it is popular all over the world.
3. The microscope made very small things larger, and scientists learned a lot using it.
4. The bifocal lens helped people to see things close to them, and it helped them to see far away.
5. The computer worked with a lot of information, and it worked quickly.

Exercise 2

1. Telecopiers are useful in large businesses, but they are expensive to buy.
2. A telephoto lens increases the size of something far away, but it isn't for close things.
3. The speaker can see the teleprompter, but the audience can't.
4. I like watching TV, but I don't like every show.
5. Teleportation is not possible today, but it's a possibility for the year 3000.

Exercise 3   Answers will vary.

Exercise 4

A. Elaine was a golfer, and Eileen was a tennis player.

Elaine lived in Chicago, and Eileen lived in Los Angeles.

Elaine was the mother of five children, and Eileen was the mother of four children.

Elaine was open and friendly, and Eileen was funny and pleasant.

B. Answers will vary.

Exercise 5   Answers will vary.

Part 5   Writing Paragraphs

Warm-Up Activity

1 and 2

Chapter Three

Part 1   Vocabulary in Context

Content Vocabulary   Answers will vary:
1. Customer services help to make shopping **easy**.
   To deliver is to take to the correct **place/person**.
2. Convenience foods are foods that are easy to **prepare**.
3. A consumer is a person who buys **things/products**.
   Products are things that consumers **buy**.
4. A retailer is a person who owns a **store**.

Subtechnical Vocabulary

1. b   3. a   5. b   7. b
2. a   4. b; a   6. c   8. b

Part 2   Reading

Warm-Up Activity

1. retailing/retail stores/stores
2. paragraph 1
3. c
4. 2, 3, 5, 1, 4
5. Examples for each of these types will vary: department stores, chain stores, supermarkets, discount houses, specialty stores.

Part 3   Understanding Through Writing

General Comprehension

1. F   2. F   3. T   4. T

Word Study

1. types
2. merchandise
3. retail outlet
4. a. customer
   b. *Consumer* is general; a *customer* usually means "a person in a store."

Sentence Study   Answers will vary:
1. The five types of retail stores are department stores, chain stores, supermarkets, discount houses, and specialty stores.
2. A drugstore is an example of a specialty store.
3. Answers will vary.
4. Answers will vary.
5. It is a convenience food.

Discourse Study
1. different types of retail stores (department stores, chain stores, super-markets, and discount houses)
2. specialty stores
3. the pecans = the pecans that farmers grow, the ones just mentioned

Exercise 1 Answers will vary.

Part 4   Getting Ready to Write Paragraphs

Recognition Exercise
1. retail stores, paper clips, grocery store, department stores, chain stores, discount houses, customer services, specialty stores, hobby shops, drugstores, barbershops, butcher shops, beauty parlors, travel agencies, convenience food, pecan pie, nut companies, candy companies, nut candies, bakery shops, candy stores, grocery stores
2. Answers will vary.
3. a great variety in the kinds and sizes of retail stores
   the giant chain with large stores throughout the nation
   everything from paper clips to tractors
4. Answers will vary.
5. many, several
6. Answers will vary.

Exercise 2 Answers will vary.

Exercise 3 Answers will vary.

Part 5   Writing Paragraphs

Warm-Up Activity
1. description   2. classification   3. description of a process

Chapter Four

Part 1   Vocabulary in Context

Content Vocabulary
1. b   3. a   5. b   7. a
2. a   4. a   6. a   8. b

Subtechnical Vocabulary
1. also
2. Answers will vary.
3. skills, education, hard work, long hours, experience, ability to work well with others, etc.
4. Answers will vary.
5. Answers will vary.
6. give
7. You join them together.

8. ice
9. a suit

Part 3 Understanding Through Writing

General Comprehension
A. 1. F   2. F   3. T   4. T   5. F
B. 1. c   2. b   3. a

Word Study
1. innovative   3. manual   5. expensive, higher costs
2. techniques   4. money problems

Sentence Study
1. b 2. a 3. c 4. c

Discourse Study
1. a computer search
2. the words that you enter into the computer, the words that you and the librarian decide on
3. two or more ideas
4. materials that are on microfilm
5. computer searches, videotape, and microfilm

Part 4 Getting Ready to Write Paragraphs

Recognition Exercise
1. currently
2. database, indices
3. Answers will vary.
4. a. parentheses: *(There is a parenthesis on both sides of a note like this. The note usually explains something in the writing.)*
   b. analyses: *look at their topics in detail to understand them*
   c. appendices: *at the end of her paper, some statistical information about her topic*

Exercise 1   Answers will vary.

Part 5 Using Two-Word Verbs

Exercise 2
1. look at   3. look over (at)   5. look after, look in on
2. look up   4. look for

Part 6 Writing Paragraphs

Warm-Up Activity
1. book   3. paragraph 5. book
2. paragraph 4. book   6. paragraph

Joining Sentences
   Hometown University Library spends thousands of dollars every year on improvements and new equipment. A recent improvement is a computerized card catalog system. This system finds books at Hometown and

other local libraries; it also shows which books are checked out. Having the right materials available is important in research. Hometown University's computerized system offers people immediate information about books, but librarians find that students continue to use the regular card catalog and go to other local libraries when a book is not on the shelf. Technology is changing research techniques in the United States, but it takes time for people to learn about the new techniques.

Chapter Five

Part 1 Vocabulary in Context

Content Vocabulary

1. a 2. b 3. a 4. b 5. a

Subtechnical Vocabulary

1–3. Answers will vary.   5. difference   7. the date/the exact date
4. only one choice   6. the boss

Part 3 Understanding Through Writing

General Comprehension

1. They have to move./The city is going to tear down their neighborhood./The city government is destroying their neighborhood.
2. It's going to be hard for everyone.
3. He's an older man. "... old like us," "all our friends for the last 23 years," in the third paragraph.
4. their friends: *But we keep thinking that all our friends for the last 23 years are going to be spread out all over the city. No more bridge on the weekends at Mac and Sally's*, and similar sentences.
5. Because the city is going to build a freeway in their neighborhood.
6. Answers may vary.

Word Study

1. they   3. spread out   5. in about three weeks,
2. comfortable   4. Mac and Sally's   in a month or so

Sentence Study   Answers will vary.

1. The little grocery store where Marge meets the other women around here will be gone.
2. We won't have the little park where I sit and talk with my friends.
3. We won't play bridge on the weekends at Mac and Sally's.
4. I hope things are better for you.

Part 4 Getting Ready to Write Letters

Recognition Exercise

1. here real soon, at our new place in a month or so
2. Answers will vary.
3. And a lot of people in this neighborhood are old like us.
4. Answers will vary.
   a. our house/our neighborhood
   b. the people in this neighborhood/these people

c. my good friends

d. approximately one month

Exercise 1

1. Brenda leaves for school at either 7:30 or 7:00./either at 7:30 or at 7:00.

2. Brenda is majoring in either physics or political science./either in physics or in political science.

3. Either her brothers or her sister is going to take some night classes.

4. Brenda is getting either straight As or As and Bs.

5. Either Brenda or her brothers are going to graduate this year.

Exercise 2   Answers will vary slightly.

1. The members are either lazy or uninterested in city business.

2. Either the mayor or the police chief can probably help.

3. Either the people are unaware, or they just don't care.

4. They either hear committee reports or form more committees.

5. The people need to either demand good work from the council members or throw the bums out.

Chapter Six

Part 1   Vocabulary in Context

Subtechnical Vocabulary

1. sunlight/sunshine/heat/energy

2. comes from

3. No, there isn't./No, there is a small amount available.

4. These different pieces of equipment work together as a system.

5. money

6. c

7. a. past   b. 1   c. use

Word Opposites

1. indirect, direct

2. rise, falls

3. a. infinite, infinite   b. finite

4. heating, cooling, b

5. nonpolluting, polluting

6. top, bottom

7. a. basic   b. complicated, basic   c. complicated

Part 2   Reading

Warm-Up Activity   3, 5, 4, 1, 2, yes

Part 3   Understanding Through Writing

General Comprehension

1. Answers will vary.

2. The sun heats the Trombe wall on the south side of the house. The heat rises and goes into the house. Cool air goes through the bottom vent and gets heated by the sun. The cycle continues.

3. plants, fossil fuels, wind power, hydroelectric power
4. a. It provides an almost infinite supply of nonpolluting energy.
   b. Today the majority of our energy sources are fossil fuels.
   c. Fossil fuels are polluting and in short supply.
   d. Nuclear energy is finite and polluting.
   e. Answers will vary: It is probably important to develop solar energy./Solar energy may be more important to develop than other energy resources./Solar energy may be better than other energy forms.

Word Study
2. radioactive   6. the basics
3. diagram   7. fusion, fission
4. illustrates   8. inexhaustible
5. principles   9. contained

Sentence Study
1. c   2. a, c   3. a   4. a, c

Discourse Study
1. the energy that plants provide for our bodies
2. fossil fuels
3. the fact that energy from the sun falls on the United States at about 600 times the current rate of consumption
4. the architect designed several solar homes last year
5. there are lots of solar heated homes in this area

Part 4   Getting Ready to Write Paragraphs

Recognition Exercise
1. It is always true. (on the earth)
2. Answers will vary.
3. at the same time, after a while

Exercise 1   Answers will vary slightly.
1. Water vapor rises into the sky.
2. The water vapor forms clouds.
3. The clouds pass over the mountains.
4. Rain falls to the mountains.
5. The rainwater returns to the lake.

Exercise 2   Answers will vary.

Part 5   Writing Paragraphs

Warm-Up Activities
A. _✓_ 1.   _✓_ 2.   _✓_ 3.   ____ 4.   ____ 5.   _✓_ 6.   _✓_ 7.

Chapter Seven

Part 1   Vocabulary in Context

Content Vocabulary
B. 1. evidence   3. accuse   5. award
   2. sue   4. jury   6. file bankruptcy

Subtechnical Vocabulary: Parts of Speech

A. 1. h 2. a 3. e, g 4. f 5. d 6. c

B. violate: verb   regulation: noun
violation: noun   regulate: verb
eliminate: verb   monopoly: noun
elimination: noun   monopolize: verb
compete: verb   drastic: adjective
competition: noun   drastically: adverb
settle: verb
settlement: noun

Part 2 Reading

Warm-Up Activity

1. yes 2. Datran and MCI 3. Harold Greene 4. by line

Part 3 Understanding Through Writing

General Comprehension

Paragraph 1: 1. a regulated monopoly
2. The Justice Department and competitors accused AT&T of monopolizing.
3. b

Paragraph 3: 1. Datran went out of business because AT&T charged a low price for its competing system (and in doing this, captured the market).
2. MCI accused AT&T of delaying its progress and lowering prices in areas of competition.
3. MCI was not able to operate efficiently and probably lost business to AT&T.
4. c
5. Answers will vary: Datran and MCI had reason to believe that AT&T did not welcome competition.

Paragraph 4: 1. c
2. Answers will vary: AT&T lost a lot of money for its anticompetitive practices./It doesn't pay to engage in anticompetitive practices.

Word Study

2. practices 3. delaying 4. authorized 5. tripled

Exercise 1

1. AT&T
2. AT&T's
3. Datran and MCI
4. at that time/in 1969
5. AT&T's
6. the fact that AT&T asked a low price for its competing system
7. Datran
8. MCI's
9. AT&T and MCI

10. AT&T
11. AT&T's
12. Datran's

Part 4   Getting Ready to Write Paragraphs

Recognition Exercise
1. the first example/Datran
2. soon afterward, then
3. in 1969, in 1976
4. after AT&T created its competing system
5. The example is AT&T.

Exercise 2   Answers will vary slightly.
1. first of all   2. secondly   3. after that (then, next)   4. in the end

Exercise 3   Answers will vary.
A. Bob and Jim drove for quite a while before they found the perfect fishing spot. They walked along the river and came to a large pool of quiet water—the best place to find hungry fish looking for food. They set down their packs quietly. At the same time, Jim asked Bob to show him what to do. **First of all**, Bob showed Jim how to put together the pieces of his portable rod. **Secondly (then, next)**, he put a larger hook on the end of his line. **Then (next, after that)** he put a worm on the hook. This was one part of fishing that he didn't enjoy. **After that (next, then)**, Jim watched Bob several times before he understood exactly how to throw out the line. **Finally**, he tried it himself. To his surprise, he caught a fish after only 10 minutes.

Part 5   Writing Paragraphs

Warm-Up Activity
1. *The purpose of the case against AT&T in the early 1980s was to break up a monopoly, but the results were more helpful to AT&T than if the corporation had actually stayed as it was.*
2. Three examples are used: *for one thing, secondly, the third result of the case.*
3. The writing is convincing because it supports the thesis with facts.
4. the first and third examples: soon afterward, after the antitrust case, at that time
5. in short
6. It could be divided at "The third result of the case ...." or at "Secondly ...."

Chapter Eight
Part 2   Vocabulary Follow-Up

Subtechnical Vocabulary: Parts of Speech
A.
1. a. No, s/he doesn't.
   b. Yes, you do.

2. a. Answers will vary: automated teller, library card, etc.
   b. reduced
3. a. Answers will vary.
   b. work with and improve
4. a. Answers will vary.
   b. Answers will vary.
5. a. the beautiful meal
   b. special
6. a. minor, unimportant
   b. Answers will vary.

B. confirm: verb   challenge: noun and verb
confirmation: noun   impressive: adjective
computerize: verb   impress: verb
computerization: noun   significant: adjective
reduction: noun   significance: noun
reduce: verb
develop: verb
development: noun

Part 3   Understanding Through Reading and Writing

General Comprehension
1. c   2. c   3. a   4. b   5. c

Word Study
2. reliable   6. passenger
3. take advantage of   7. put pressure on
4. effect   8. handled
5. result   9. provided the solution

Sentence Study
1. b   2. b   3. a   4. b

Discourse Study
1. There were several [reasons], but the source of change was the invention of the jet engine.
2. a related effect, a third result
3. in summary

Part 4   Getting Ready to Write a Short Composition

2. C   3. E   4. E   5. E   6. E   7. E

Exercise 1
1. Small farmers cannot compete with large-scale farming, so many farmers are going out of business.
   Many small farmers are going out of business because they cannot compete with large-scale farming.

2. Research showed that smoking was a significant cause, so many people stopped smoking.
   Many people stopped smoking because research showed that smoking was a significant cause.
3. There is a lot of research in the field, so innovations in language teaching are common.
   Innovations in language teaching are common because there is a lot of research in the field.
4. The huge amount of materials is impossible to handle manually, so libraries are computerizing.
   Libraries are computerizing because the huge amount of materials is impossible to handle manually.
5. It takes longer to create fossil fuels than to use them, so they are in short supply these days.
   Fossil fuels are in short supply these days because it takes longer to create them than to use them.

Exercise 2   Answers will vary.

Chapter Nine

Part 1   Vocabulary in Context

Subtechnical Vocabulary
1. businessman
2. a lot of
3. mostly
4. extraordinary
5. probable cause
6. because of
7. the restaurants mentioned second
8. in addition to
9. money

Part 2   Reading

Warm-Up Activity
1. 7 out of 10
2. $14.3 billion
3. Burger King and Wendy's
4. more than 140,000

Part 3   Vocabulary Follow-Up

Parts of Speech
1. a   3. a   5. b   7. a   9. a
2. b   4. b   6. a   8. b

Part 4   Understanding Through Writing

General Comprehension
1. a, c
2. c
3. one of the reasons, another reason, an additional factor

4. a, b
5. a, c

Word Study

2. singles   5. urban
3. additional   6. existing
4. factor   7. appetite
                8. beefed up

Sentence Study

1. a   2. c   3. b   4. a

Discourse Study Answers will vary.

Part 5 Getting Ready to Write Paragraphs

Recognition Exercise

1. a great deal of, noncount nouns, noncount
2. companies, count
3. more than seven out of ten
4. one of the reasons

Exercise 1

1. a paper   4. company   7. business
2. a play   5. times   8. change
3. a quality   6. service

Exercise 2 Answers will vary.

Part 6 Using Suffixes

Exercise 3

1. commutes, commute   5. experiments, experiment
2. diversify, diversification   6. estimate, estimate
3. expand, expansion   7. experienced, experiences
4. representation, represents   8. creates, creation

Chapter Ten

Part 1 Vocabulary in Context

Content Vocabulary

1–3. Answers will vary.
   4. September, December
   5. a
   6. b
   7. a
   8. a
   9. added to

Part 2 Reading

Warm-Up Activity

1. T 2. IE 3. F 4. F 5. F

Part 3 Vocabulary Follow-Up

Subtechnical Vocabulary

B. 1. take for granted 5. minimum 9. consider
2. take place 6. emphasize 10. vary
3. respectively 7. per
4. maximum 8. set

Part 4 Understanding Through Writing

General Comprehension

1. b
2. Banks are not allowed to pay more than the maximum interest rate. Banks are not allowed to branch freely.
3. with savings accounts, as for checking accounts
4. b
5. b

Exercise 1

1. The majority of banks pay interest four times a year.
2. It is important to determine the most helpful services before opening an account.
3. You can't assume that every bank gives the best interest rate on savings accounts.
4. Commercial banks currently provide many more services thanks to computers.

Exercise 2

1. the maximum rate on savings accounts
2. the government
3. banks
4. the (banking) services
5. other banks
6. a bank
7. additional services
8. the services of banks (banks' services)

Part 5 Getting Ready to Write Paragraphs

Recognition Exercise

1. b
2. It doesn't allow them to branch freely into other states.
3. it is a good idea

Exercise 3

1. The election results weren't available, nor were the trends clear.
2. He didn't state a choice, nor did he discuss his ideas about it.
3. The bank president didn't look at the document, nor did he discuss it with anyone.
4. She didn't think noise pollution was related to her work, nor did she think it was a large-scale problem.

5. My bank doesn't have free checking accounts, nor does it have drive-up windows.

Exercise 4   Answers will vary.

Exercise 5   Answers will vary.

Chapter Eleven

Part 2   Vocabulary Follow-Up

Content Vocabulary
B. 1. background   4. shot   7. being
   2. film   5. space station 8. monster
   3. space   6. model   9. spaceship

Part 3   Understanding Through Writing

General Comprehension
1. logical   2. logical   3. illogical   4. illogical

Word Study
2. make use of   5. technique   9. movie-goers
3. range   6. giant   10. stimulate
4. depends on   7. in wide use 11. the public
                 8. is able to

Sentence Study   Answers will vary.
1. Special effects are achieved through the use of **a wide variety of techniques.**
2. The use of many special effects **contributes importantly to the popularity of science fiction movies.**
3. Filmmakers will continue to make movies with special effects because **these films are very successful.**

Discourse Study
1. method   2. drawings   3. this machine   4. part

Part 4   Getting Ready to Write Paragraphs

Recognition Exercise
1. explain the previous statement
2. another technique, still another technique
3. The film printer, for example, was developed in the 1930s. Another innovation is the flex camera, which was developed for *Star Wars*.
4. It makes predictions.

Exercise 1   Answers will vary.

Exercise 2   Answers will vary.

Exercise 3   Answers will vary.

Chapter Twelve

Part 1 Vocabulary in Context

Content Vocabulary

1. g 4. e 7. d
2. c 5. f
3. a 6. h

Part 2 Reading

Warm-Up Activity

Paragraph 1: Because these tests are commonly used to help determine entrance eligibility, students should learn about the factors that affect scores on standardized tests.

Paragraph 2: Standardized tests are similar to one another in many ways.

Paragraph 3: There are differences among tests as well.

Paragraph 4: In short, there are many things you can do to improve your score on a standardized test.

Paragraph 5: Reading the test directions seems simple, but it is more important than many people realize.

Part 3 Vocabulary Follow-Up

Subtechnical Vocabulary

1. probable
2. consider the facts and form an opinion
3. direct attention to
4. general statement
5. find
6. is different from
7. suggest
8. looking critically at

Part 4 Understanding Through Writing

General Comprehension

1. S 2. I 3. I 4. I 5. S 6. N

Sentence Study Answers will vary.

1. It is important for students to understand that **various standardized tests focus on different skills**.
2. There are quite a few similarities **among standardized tests**.
3. The computer lowers a score for **wrong answers**.
4. To maximize your chances for a good score, you **should give yourself plenty of time to prepare for a standardized test**.

Discourse Study

2, 4, 5, 1, 3

I. General Information about Standardized Tests
   A. Necessary for most students
   B. Importance of learning about factors that affect scores
      1. kinds of questions and answers
      2. skill area emphasis

II. Similarities among Standardized Tests
   A. Timed exams for large groups

   B. Multiple choice—scored by computer _____

   C. Require strong reading and vocabulary
   D. Thinking skills/tasks on standardized tests

      1. making judgments _____

      2. drawing conclusions _____

      3. identifying what has been implied

      4. summarizing and making generalizations _____

      5. determining meanings through context

      6. identifying what was not stated or implied _____

III. Differences among Standardized Tests _____

   A. Penalty for guessing differs from test to test
   B. Explanatory example of penalty for guessing

IV. How to Prepare for a Standardized Test
   A. Start early

   B. Make sure of location _____

   C. Get a *Bulletin of Information*

   D. Use a study guide _____

V. Read the Directions _____

Part 5   Getting Ready to Write a Composition

1. G   3. G   5. S   7. S
2. S   4. S   6. G

Recognition Exercise

1. most students, standardized tests, commonly, factors, kinds of questions and answers, skill areas
2. standardized tests, in many ways
3. to begin with, secondly, another similarity, still another similarity
4. a
5. final

Index to Subtechnical and Content Vocabulary

Index

Imperatives
  in direct language, 139-40
  to give advice, 137
Implication and direct statement, 158
Indenting paragraphs, 27
Inferences, 144-45
Informal writing style, 65
Irregular plurals, from Latin and Greek, 51

Joining ideas, 7
Joining sentences, 57-58

Letter writing, 68-69

Main ideas
  finding, 33, 49, 90-91, 105, 155
  introduction, 27-28
  restating, 111
Main points
  giving, 107, 162
  listing, 70
  summarizing, 107, 162

Narration, 93-95, 162
Negative prefixes (un-, non-, im-, in-), 9
Noncount nouns. See Nouns
Nor, 136-37
Noun modifiers
  adjectives, 37-38
  noun + noun, 37
  prepositional phrases, 37-38
Nouns
  and verbs with identical form, 126
  noncount, 81, 122-24
  reference to. See Reference
  that are count and noncount, 122-23

One/s, for reference, 135
Or, 65
Orientation guide, 59
Other/another, as subject signals, 148
Outlining, 159-60

Paragraphs
  form, 27-28, 57
  function, 75, 119-20
  introduction, 5

one topic per, 68
organization of, 27-28, 40, 82-83, 165
types of, 40, 105
  argumentation, 98-99, 128
  cause and effect, 105, 111-12
  classification, 10-12, 40, 55
  conclusion, 150-51
  description, 40, 41, 55-56
  description of a process, 40, 83-84, 140, 162
  explanation, 28, 40, 55-56
  narrative, 40, 93-95, 99
  prediction, 151-52
Paraphrasing, 134, 146, 158-59
Parts of speech, 87-88, 103-4, 117-19
  noun-forming suffixes, 126
  nouns and verbs with identical form, 126
Past tense, in narration, 93-95
Periods, 6
Personalizing, 65, 92
Place expressions, 21-22
Plan to. See Verbs, with future meaning
Plurals. See Irregular plurals
Pre-articles, with fractions and percentages, 124
Predicting content, 3-4, 19, 101
Predictive conclusions, with will, 148
Prefixes (un-, non-, im-, in-), 9
Prepositional phrases, 37-38
Present progressive, 51
Present tense, 80-81, 161
Process, description of a, 40, 83-84, 140, 162
Pronouns. See Reference, to people and things
Punctuation. See names of marks

Quantity expressions
  a great deal of, a great number of, 123-24
  for reference, 121-22
  in generalizations, 161
  pre-articles, with fractions and percentages, 124
Question mark, 6
Quotations, 163-64

Reasons, 23, 108-9
Reference
  noun phrase
    to people and things, 92
    to time and place, 92-93
    with one/s, 135-36
    with quantity expressions and
      numbers, 121-22
    with synonyms, 147

with *this, that, these, those, the*, 36-37, 51,
    79, 93, 136
  sentence, 79, 93
Restatement. *See* Synonymous sentences,
  Paraphrasing
Revising, 30, 43, 71, 100, 114, 128, 140, 153,
  166
Rhetorical questions, 105

Scanning, 89, 116
Semicolon, 22, 137
Sentence reference. *See* Reference
Sequence expressions, 93-95, 162
Series of actions, 81
Should, to give advice, 137
Skimming, 33-34, 75, 101, 130-31
So, 108-09
Specifics, 8, 12-13, 21, 107, 133-34, 160-61, 162
Style
  academic, 28, 92, 148
  expository, 28
  informal, 51, 65
  narrative, 93-95
  personalized, 65, 92
Subject signals
  introduction, 107
  summary, 162
  with forms of *other*, 148
Subtechnical vocabulary, introduction, 2
Suffixes (*-ation, -tion, -sion*), 126
Summary statements, 107, 162
Synonymous sentences, 50, 78-79, 106, 120-21
Synonyms, 147, 157-58

The, for reference, 36-37
The fact that, in sentence reference, 79

Then
  as a sequence expression, 94-95
  for reference to time, 92
There, for reference to place, 92-93
There + be
  in general statements, 38, 107, 161
  with quantity expressions, 38
Thesis
  cause and effect, 111
  supporting a, 97-98, 111, 128
This
  for noun phrase reference, 36-37, 51, 79, 93, 136
  for sentence reference, 79, 93
Time expressions, 21-22, 51, 80
Titles, 21, 166
Topics
  as expressed by a topic sentence, 27, 98
  introducing, 107
  limiting, 54-55
  locating, 33
Topic sentences
  introduction, 12, 27-28
  writing, 29, 39
Two-word verbs, with *look*, 53

Verbs. *See also* names of tenses
  and nouns with identical form, 126
  imperatives, 137, 139-40
  with future meaning, 148

Will, 148
Word opposites. *See* Antonyms

Yet, 136-37